THINK LIKE A BANKER... *AND FLIP DEBT ON ITS HEAD*

Includes the example of 3 uses for every $1

WILL MORAN

Think Like a Banker
Copyright © 2019 by Will Moran

Tellwell Talent
www.tellwell.ca

ISBN
978-0-2288-0435-2 (Hardcover)
978-0-2288-0433-8 (Paperback)
978-0-2288-0434-5 (eBook)

For Sue Moran,
my wife, best friend, and the greatest love of my life

Reader Reviews

Finally, a book that properly addresses the pressing issue of personal debt we are facing in Canada today. Where traditional financial planning makes note of, yet, does little to address this issue, Will Moran provides his readers with a real solution. I was captivated by the simplicity in which Will communicates Infinite Banking; taking a complicated financial strategy and breaking it down to the 'you and me' level to conceptually help people walk through how Infinite Banking can help them regardless if they are wealthy already or not.

Ashley Lalonde
The Wise Banker

"Measured Wisdom" best describes this book and why it should be read carefully – move over Dave – make room for Will!"

Larry T Wells,
Barrister & Solicitor, Juris Doctor

As a dealership finance rep I often see people buried in their bills and I cannot give them better advice, as it goes against my job to make money for my employer. This information is a revolution in personal finance, even if the only thing you did was use it as a tool to make your vehicle purchases. It would build your retirement nest-egg by HUNDREDS OF THOUSANDS by using compound interest properly.

Shannon
Finance Rep for a H@*/# Dealership

I appreciate the Canadian angle and content that Will's book offers. It was an easy read and makes very good sense. It took me through concrete examples of financial situations. It is helping me complete my due diligence and I am asking more intelligent questions. In that way, I feel 100% comfortable with my decision to proceed as I have already walked through all the uses, advantages and disadvantages of a personal banking/financing/retirement system which is based on a platform with many benefits

Amanda Loch
Consultant, Entrepreneur

Will Moran brings to light an interesting way to not only save and diversify your money, but also for 'borrowing' money while making money.

Ashley Whyte
Edmonton

GENERAL DISCLAIMER

TABLE OF CONTENTS

ACKNOWLEDGEMENTS

Although my name is listed as the author, it did not happen without the thorough work and diligent efforts and the encouragement of great people in my life.

I would not be writing this book if I did not discover the Infinite Banking Concept (IBC), by R. Nelson Nash, quite by accident. Three people, all within a week's span, coincidentally asked me if I had ever heard of this concept. One person, a good friend of mine, asked if I would recommend it as a financial strategy for him and his wife. That was over 6 years ago. Maybe there's no such thing as coincidence. Could it be instead that when the student is ready the teachers will appear? I just couldn't ignore it then and immediately bought the book and read it through in one evening.

I would not be where I am today if I had not picked up the book and absorbed its timeless message. To R. Nelson Nash, who created the Infinite Banking Concept and realized it was something of great value before anyone else recognized it, I owe a great debt of gratitude (see my tribute to Nelson in the back of this book); and to the people behind the Nelson Nash Institute such as David Stearns, Dr. Robert Murphy and Carlos Lara, these people are the reason any of us have ever heard of IBC.

I owe a huge debt of gratitude to my editor, Ann Marie Downey, who really gets the concept as evidenced by her nifty, and always dead-on, editing re-arrangements. Also, to Richard Canfield, who is a friend, a great guy, and who is regularly calling me and keeping me in the loop and what's new in the IBC world. I've never met anyone quite like Richard who is so thorough in everything he does. To people like Ashley LaLonde, Mike Sidhu, Winnie Lua, Jayson Lowe, Glen Zacher (who sold me the book in the first place), Dale Moffat and many others I owe a lot of thanks for their insight and passion when discussing this topic. To Chris Bay, Mike Everett, and Chris Gerriets from Lawrence, Kansas who insisted I attend their bootcamp and where I learned so much, I thank you. Thanks to Mike Everette for being a pillar in the Nelson Nash Institute; to Chris Bay for always sharing his brilliant ideas, and to Chris Gerriets for the most concise summary of "What is The Infinite Banking Concept?" displayed on their website, I have ever read. Thanks to the three of you for letting me borrow your ideas!

To the many authors who have written before me, and who are listed in the back of this book, I couldn't have had the understanding or clarity without reading and absorbing the material and wealth of knowledge that exists in their pages. To everyone listed, I say a heartfelt "thank you" for sharing and expanding the information surrounding this topic.

INTRODUCTION

"Tell me and I forget. Teach me and I remember. Involve me and I learn."

—Benjamin Franklin

THE EXPERTS

No one needs to hear more "expert" financial advice. Listening to the financial "experts" is one of the reasons many Canadians struggle in their attempts to overcome the mountain of debt they are besieged with today. For many people, whether they are starting out in life and beginning to raise a family or whether they have been doing so for years, or even decades, are finding themselves still struggling with the same roadblocks they started out with. They are still neck deep in debt, with a mortgage, a car loan, or two, and a line of credit on top of that, and still can't see the light of day much better than they did decades before. At best, they are managing their debt, but have been offered little help in the way of proven strategies to finance all those things they purchase and still enable them to save for retirement. Never in our lifetime will as many people continue to have debt issues like they do now as they enter into their 30's, their 40's, their 50's, their 60's, and even into their 70's, holding them in financial bondage to the financial institutions they deal with.

FINANCING INCLUDES EVERYONE

We would all like to take more control over the financing and banking functions in our everyday lives. Whether you pay cash for everything you buy, or not, you are still financing. We finance everything we buy. Either we borrow money and pay interest to someone else to buy it, or we pay cash and give up the interest we could have earned had we invested it. *Pay up, or give up!* How can we link these two opposites together and pay for the things we want without giving up the earning potential of our capital, AND without paying interest to a system that doesn't benefit us?

In this book, I will present the information you need to do exactly that and effectively flip debt on its head. By the end of the book you will be asking yourself why you hadn't heard of this before. I get asked this all the time. Depending on your age, you may ask, "Where were you 20 years ago?" Be prepared though, you will need to put aside much of what you have been taught in the way of financial products and services and gain a new perspective on how to handle your personal economies (Ermen 8).

Why? Because traditional financial models ignore two vital factors I will address in this book:

1. 99% of people need to *finance* one or more purchases, in some way, shape or form, but are going about it in the least efficient way; and
2. 168% above what they earn is what the average Canadian spends. (Ashley LaLonde, *The Wise Banker*)

DEEPER INDEBTEDNESS

The increased cost of vehicles and homes has far outpaced the rise in incomes over the past two to three decades. This has made the amount of money flowing away from us for financing these purchases an increasingly bigger problem. Indebtedness levels today are monstrous, resulting in more people having more commitments to bankers and lenders than ever before. Traditional financial advice does a poor job of addressing this issue.

FINANCIAL INDUSTRY: NOT HELPING

The traditional financial products and advice pushed at people today, and backed by financial gurus and industry giants, do not take the pressing issue of *personal debt* into account to the extent required. Time and again, we see headlines of how people are drowning in debt, and while making note of it, traditional financial planning programs do little to address it.

Is there any incentive for banks and other lending institutions to initiate the needed change, since they are the ones making steady profits through fees and interest charges, while we, the ones borrowing the funds, call it "cheap money?" Hardly!

BEING TOLD TO CUT BACK

Many of my younger clients do not trust the market and are more skeptical of it than their parents were. They look back at the huge market swings of the last 25 or 30 years and shutter at how little control they have over it and how few real gains they have seen.

They look at their mortgage statements and cringe at the vast amount of interest charges they are regularly paying and shake their heads— knowing they will never see that money again. On top of that, they feel helpless to do anything about it. Even though interest rates are low, the volume of interest they pay out is high due to the enormity of their mortgages.

They do not want to give up their holiday trailer or boat, as they are being told to do by financial gurus. Why should they? They got it in the first place to create lasting memories their children will take with them into the future. Family memories: these are important to them. The only answer from the gurus is to cut these things out.

The good news is, *they don't have to!* What they must be willing to do however, is to learn to think differently than how they were taught.

"You can lead a human to knowledge, but you can't make them think."

—Mary Jo Ermin, author of *Wealth Without the Bank*

WE NEED A DYNAMIC NEW STRATEGY

What we need is a dynamic new strategy of proven success to *finance* those things we purchase, and a new way to *save* for our retirement. For many people, the current way of financing and saving is not working efficiently, if at all. The perfect Canadian life of having a good job or business our whole life, and retiring with a *guaranteed* pension, is gone. The perfect Canadian life of retiring with a large portfolio free of risk is gone. The perfect Canadian life of paying off our house in our mid-thirties or early forties is an impossible dream for most.

It has been estimated that, for the average person, 34% of every disposable dollar paid out goes to debt services (i.e., loan interest and fees). That is a loss $0.34 of every $1.00, and all that money goes to someone else! Ironically, this ratio stays the same regardless of how much money people make. It is human nature that the more we make, the more we spend.

Assume the average person is trying to save 10% of their disposable income (which is a stretch, since the average person comes nowhere close to that). That means we have a 3.4 to 1 ratio of interest paid out compared to savings. In other words, we are paying out 3.4 times more in interest than we are actually saving!

If you were to have a conversation with the average person saving for their retirement, they would spend all their time talking about the high rate of return they are getting on their investments (i.e., their savings). What they do not mention, or may even realize, is what their savings is *earning* is getting eaten up by the interest they are *paying* to the companies they are indebted to. This part gets overlooked. What a tragedy! But that is how they have learned to conduct their financial affairs.

R. NELSON NASH

The financial book that has had the biggest and best impact on my professional life is *Becoming Your Own Banker** by R. Nelson Nash. In it, he introduces "The Infinite Banking Concept" (IBC). In the first few pages of his book he states if all the wealth in the world was distributed equally among all the people in the world, within ten years 97% of all the wealth would be back in the hands of 3% of the people who control wealth. I do not know if the numbers are accurate, but the notion is undeniable. Wealthy people think differently than average people.

Most of us have been conditioned to think certain ways and to follow given "industry standards" in the financial world when tending to our personal economy. But is this getting us to where we want to go? Garret B. Gunderson, author of *"Killing Sacred Cows"* asks, "if only a minority of people are wealthy, why do we follow what the majority of people do financially?"

I'll admit when I first read Nelson Nash's book and understood the central concept of what he was saying and knowing he had become somewhat of a celebrity because of it, I wondered why everyone was not jumping on the bandwagon and doing what he was saying to do. But new ideas are not always readily accepted. While most people, after reading *Becoming Your Own Banker*, look at their own financial world through entirely different lenses than ever before, the book has been criticized and downgraded by people whose industries and livelihoods would potentially suffer because of it. A quick scan of the internet will reveal this. And, it has been written off by financial companies that do not offer the products he is recommending. Insiders of our industry can tell you that.

Perhaps the wealthy minded catch on to ideas quicker and rely more on their own judgements, and less on the judgements of others, when they encounter an idea whose time has come. According to Arthur Schopenhauer, a 19th century philosopher, "All truth passes through three stages. First, it is ridiculed. Second, it is violently opposed. Third, it is accepted as being self-evident."

MY MISSION

I made it my mission, after reading and re-reading Nash's book countless times, referring to it regularly, and giving away hundreds of copies to my clients, that I would communicate its timeless message to inspire anyone who wanted to take back control of their personal economy and steer their own financial future. I believe that if people know about the financially beneficial message Mr. Nash has for them, most people will want to act on it immediately.

Many people blame their financial advisors for their financial foibles, when they really should be taking the blame themselves. Nobody cares more about your financial future than you do. It is foolish to think otherwise. It is like thinking the teacher will raise your kid better than you will.

There used to be a time when the company you worked at for 30 to 40 years would take care of you when you retired. They would present you with a gold watch and an even more golden pension plan that would pay you an indexed income for the rest of your life. You did not even have to be financially literate or understand how pensions worked. It was taken care of for you. Those days are gone. Now, it is up to you. You cannot afford to remain financially illiterate. If you allow banks and financial advisors to take control of your entire personal economy, they will take you for a ride.

My hope is to make you more aware of your financial environment and the forces that are keeping so many Canadians from achieving their financial dreams. It begins with how you think. You will then be able to turn your finances around in your favor.

Thinking differently, and incorporating new ideas into what we already know is progress, has helped countless individuals, and it will help you. With every email I sign off on, these are the words that follow: *"Changing Thinking, Changing Lives."* If you're open to it, this book can change your thinking AND change your life.

CHAPTER

ONE

CONTROLLING YOUR FINANCIAL ENVIRONMENT

Here in Canada, the perfect life of financial success is getting harder to envision. For most people, married, raising two or three young kids, the thought of having a successful early retirement is too far down the road to imagine. Parkinson's Law states that even if both parents are working and they have a good household income, their "expenses rise to equal income." So true!

Like many of us, a couple's income is up against expenses, such as paying down a mortgage, a car loan, maybe a line of credit or a credit card with an ongoing balance. As well, a couple's combined income needs to go toward paying for a whole list of monthly expenses. Some of these expenses are fixed costs, including food, utilities, heating, cell phone and internet. Other expenses are somewhat discretionary, such as clothing, entertainment, recreation, and kids' expenses, like school activities, sports equipment and registration costs for soccer, hockey, dancing or other sports. And, the list goes on.

On top of that, many financial gurus tell us we should be putting away 10% of our income for retirement. If we tithe, then possibly another 10% is going there. An additional 30% to 50% of our hard-earned income goes toward paying income, property and sales taxes. What's left? For many, not much!

FACING A HEADWIND

Is it any wonder Canadians are facing such a headwind when trying to save for their future? For many, the thought of saving 10% is only a dream. This book will give you specific financial solutions to these issues that traditional financial advice, including big investment firms, banks, and lending institutions are *unwilling*, or *unable*, to provide. Please read on.

CONDITIONED BEHAVIOUR

> *"If you listen to the masses, you'll end up like the masses."*
>
> —Unknown

The status quo is not a pretty picture. Many people are running their lives on automatic pilot and are not making direction changes when necessary. They just keep doing the same old things that are not getting them anywhere better fast. It is akin to driving at night, with no headlights, on a secondary road that has no signage. Would you even know where you were going?

Are you running on autopilot? Are you conditioned to think like everyone else? When it comes to our money we are conditioned to think we need the banks to purchase things and the stock market to retire with. But conditioned thinking leaves little room for our own thinking. And given the state of people's finances these days, as I outlined above, it no longer serves us to simply follow the crowd. Statistics show people are plunging deeper in debt every year.

The famous sociologist, Ivan Pavlov, demonstrated that dogs could be conditioned to salivate every time a bell is rung. Each time the dogs were about to be fed, he would ring a bell. Eventually, the dogs began to salivate profusely whenever the bell rang, knowing food would soon follow. Then, the sociologist began ringing the bell at times the dogs were not getting fed. Whether their food arrived or not, when hearing the bell, the dogs would still salivate. They had been conditioned to do so. We humans are not so different. Through conditioning we, too, follow suit.

So, while traditional roads to financial success may not lead to the same rewards they once did, many people are still following that same road. Just like Pavlov's dogs, they are conditioned to take the same actions with their finances, regardless of whether or not the reward will arrive.

It's like being stuck in a rut. Imagine driving your car down a road with deep ruts. The deeper the ruts, the harder it is to get out! This is where many of us are today. We are told to go without, save up and pay cash for the big things we buy, use the bank's money when necessary because it is cheap, and save up for retirement by investing in the stock market. To use a Dr. Phil line, "How's that working for you?"

ASKING DIFFERENT QUESTIONS

Financial gurus *tell* us what we should do. We do not necessarily question whether the advice is good or bad. We simply do what everyone else is doing, expecting our results will somehow be different. Many times, the advice comes from the talking heads in the media who are guests on broadcasting shows. Other times, it is the people who have been "ordained" to give financial advice outside their area of expertise.

I cannot tell you the number of times clients ask me to meet with their CPA or lawyer to verify the information I am presenting them is valid. It does not seem to matter whether or not these professionals have expertise in this area. These well-meaning professionals have somehow been given the distinction of "all knowing" and some of them act like they are. However, while each of our industries have professional standards, and annual continuing education requirements to meet, it is surprising how little some tax and legal professionals know about our industry.

Sometimes, my meetings with these professionals are very short. Like a rusty faucet, their minds just won't open enough to let anything fresh flow through. In short, they have the "arrival syndrome". If someone is afflicted with the arrival syndrome, they think they already know everything there is to know about my industry, including the tax advantages and the preservation of capital we can offer. Often, it ends up we know more about their industry than they know about ours.

Other times, when I meet these professionals, our meetings are collaborative and open whole new areas of insight for each of us. As the light bulbs turn on, we start to see solutions for our clients that neither of us had envisioned before. With egos aside, the client is the biggest benefactor. This also often leads to receiving good referrals from them, resulting in even more people finding out about my industry, and in particular, IBC, and that is my personal mission. So, while some accountants, tax professionals, and lawyers are afflicted with the arrival syndrome, most are not.

Thomas Edison said: "Five percent of the people think; ten percent of the people think they think; and the other eighty-five percent would rather die than think." As my friend and author, as well as a practitioner of IBC, Mary Jo Irmen says:

> When we look at those 85%, are they conditioned to not ask questions, or have they truly arrived and believe their thinking days are over? There is a big difference between not questioning and knowing it all. Often those who question, have given in to conditioned thinking but are still very teachable.

If you are reading this book, I am guessing you are one of those people who is at least ready to question the financial advice you are getting.

CHAPTER
TWO

LET'S TALK ABOUT BANKS

Let's talk about banks for a minute. Do you think their goal is to grow your money or have you grow their money? In other words, would they rather pay you, or have you pay them?

Banks are in business to make money, just like any other business. They are not in business to be your friend. They provide a service. They want you to borrow money—lots of it—but they do not want to be left holding property if you default. They will take every measure to prevent this from happening. They want cash flow! That is their life blood.

After 2008, when the housing bubble burst in the United States, Canada made major changes to how banks could lend money. You now need a bigger down payment to buy a home and the lending practices are much tighter. Banks need the house payment, not the house.

But many practices have not changed. The more cash flow the banks have the more money they can lend out—many times more than what they have on deposit—which allows banks to create more cash flow coming in. We can all learn a lot from watching how banks do business. They never let cash just sit and stagnate. The more cash they have the more they lend. Truth be known, banks would rather you never get out of the debt cycle. They prefer you keep racking up debt like a shopper on steroids—taking out more and more loans—than becoming debt-free and getting out of bondage. This is even more true of credit card companies and second-rate lenders.

When you make a deposit to a bank, is it an asset or a liability for the bank? Most people believe it is an *asset*. The truth is, taking deposits is a *liability* for the bank because they *owe* you money. On the other hand, when you borrow money from the bank, you owe *them*, so it is an *asset* to them. You are essentially working for them and paying them interest. The sad part is that you will never see that money again. It is a permanent one-way wealth transfer to the bank. It is gone.

SORRY! YOU'RE DENIED!

Even though it is an asset to the banks, getting approved for a loan is not always easy. I know people who have been denied money when they have needed it most. Even having been loyal bank customers for decades, and having lots of equity in their homes, they were turned down for loans.

Just because you have equity in your home, you are not guaranteed access to that money. Banks can turn anyone down. Many banks will deny you a loan if you have started a business and do not have more than a few years of financials to show them. Or, if by some fluke, your credit rating has a low number, you will also be denied a loan. If you are retired or have lost your job, the banks will think twice about you too. You are too much of a risk to the banks.

Even if you feel this does not apply to you because you are financially well-off and have a great track record, you will still have to prove to the bank that you can make your repayment and will not default. Good credit and repayment history are not guarantees you will get the money.

Ironically, when a bank or other lender does a credit check to see if you have a "good credit rating," that action itself can lower your credit score. So, shopping around for the best rate can actually result in you getting denied a loan, since each potential lender will check, and thus, effect your credit score!

HIGH-INTEREST-RATE ENVIRONMENTS

In the early 1980s, my parents sold the family farm and put the money from that sale into Guaranteed Investment Certificates (GICs). This was during the high-interest-rate days for GICs, which at that time were paying an astounding 13%! It's hard to imagine that kind of return in today's environment.

So, what did that do for my parents? Well, the Rule of 72, which was discovered by none other than Albert Einstein, says that when you divide "72" by the interest rate, the resulting number is the number of years it will take for your money to *double*. (72 / 13% = 5.5) So, if you ignore tax, it only took five and a half years for my parents' money to double! Can you imagine? Because of the interest it earned and kept earning, even after tax, it set my parents up with a good retirement income (which was a blessing, since our family was not wealthy).

During that same period of time, banks were *lending* money at 21%! This left the buyer of our farm with hefty mortgage payments. Since the bank was paying out 13% on the GIC to my parents, while lending out at 21% to the buyer of our farm, it may have looked, at first glance, like the bank was making a spread of 8%. That was not actually the case. When you break it down into actual dollars, you can see why.

Suppose you deposit $100 in the bank and they are paying 13%. This means they are paying you $13 to "rent" your money for a year. At the same time, if I need $100 and the bank is charging me 21%, this means they will charge me $21 to "sublet" your $100 to me. Do you follow?

So, they are going to "rent" from you for $13 and "sublet" to me for $21. The difference is $8. What is the bank's markup of your money? Their profit margin of ($8) / cost ($13) x 100 = percentage markup (61.5%). They are making 61.5% off your money!

Think about it another way. If I am a retailer and my cost for an extension cord is $13 and I sell it for $21, that is a 61.5% markup (i.e., ($21 - $13) / ($13) x 100 = 61.5%). The bank is like any retail business. All they are doing is marking up money.

LOW-INTEREST-RATE ENVIRONMENTS

Let's look at what banks are making today in this low-interest-rate environment. Today, a five-year GIC may pay you only 1.42% annual interest, but the cost to borrow money is also low at 3.42%. It looks like the bank is only making 2%, since they are paying out at 1.42% and lending out at 3.42%. *But, looks can be deceiving.* The profit for the bank is actually so much higher in a low-interest-rate environment. Here, the markup for the bank is an astounding <u>140.85%</u>!

$$(3.42\% - 1.42\%) / 1.42\% \times 100 = 140.85\%$$

Thus, in low-interest-rate environments, it is easier for banks to make higher profits, while looking like they are not. Low interest rates are a big win for the banks, but not for those of us who are trying to save.

But all is not lost. As I will discuss in the next chapter, there are more lucrative places where your money can reside, where you have more accessibility, growth, and options, and where it is just as safe.

THE REAL CULPRIT: VOLUME OF INTEREST

In today's low-interest-rate environment (which will certainly increase— we have had three increases in the past year as of the writing of this book) we have been conditioned to think money is cheap. The going bank rate for your mortgage may be as low as 2.69%. Your car loan may be advertised at 4.99%. But it is not the annual interest rate that should concern us. The real culprit is the *volume of interest.*

As an example, let's look at buying a car. A 5% annual interest rate charged on a $30,000 car purchase over seven years adds $5,555.83 in interest. The *volume of interest* in this case is 18.5% ($5,555.83 / $30,000 x 100 = 18.5%)!

For a typical mortgage, the volume of interest is much higher because of the length of the amortization period. In the first five years of a typical mortgage loan, with lending rates now rising, the volume of interest to principal paid will be much higher. For example, for a 25-year mortgage in the amount of $400,000, at a fixed rate of 4%, with monthly payments of $1902.07, the borrower will pay $114,124 in the first five years, but only $38,403 of that amount will go to reduce the loan. This means that in five years, *$75,721 will go to interest.* Divide that interest by the total amount paid ($75,721 / $114,114 x 100) and you find that 66.3% *of every dollar paid out goes to the cost of financing!* So, it is not a stretch for us to see that the average Canadian pays out $0.34 of every dollar as an *interest expense!*

Let's assume you are *saving* $0.10 of every dollar of your disposable income (which is twice the average savings rate in Canada) and you are paying, in interest, $0.34 of every dollar of your disposable income. That would mean you have a 3.4 to 1 ratio of interest paid out compared to savings! This is what we call a *headwind.*

In this scenario, while you are doing your best to get ahead, you are actually going backwards, in the grand scheme of things. When we do the math, what we hoped would be a $0.10 savings from every dollar has turned into a $0.24 loss from every dollar. (In chapter eight I will describe how to turn a *headwind* into a *tailwind*). On top of this, you are also paying a boatload of tax, which ends up taking at least $0.30 of every dollar. Is it any wonder we struggle to get ahead and save for our retirement?

But let's imagine having that money flowing to us, instead of to the banks, in a tax-exempt plan we own and control! What opportunities could you take advantage of and how could this improve your personal economy?

The Infinite Banking Concept is for individuals, like you and me, to take back control of the financing and banking functions in our everyday lives, turning a headwind into a tailwind, and to recapture the lost-opportunity costs—the costs of either paying up or giving up interest, so to speak—that are plainly robbing us of our future. The traditional planning advice given to Canadians today is doing little to help us in this critical area.

WHAT'S THE SOLUTION?

It is one thing to define the problem, but what is the *solution?* How do you reverse this trend? Banking is a necessary function in our everyday lives. We could not live and enjoy the standard of living we have today without banking. But what is it doing to us?

As Lara, Murphy and Nash (2018, 51) note, the bankers have all but taken over the banking function in life and people have become "financial slaves." The remedy must be at the *individual level*, so, they implore us to *become our own source of financing*. This can be done by anyone. The wealthy in Canada have done it for generations. The good news is you do not have to be wealthy to start living profitably, while enjoying a peaceful, stress-free lifestyle.

Lara, Murphy, and Nash (2018, 54) sum it up this way:

> Banking is all about accumulating money and making loans to people who will pay them back. You should be the ideal customer of your system. You should make loans to yourself—and pay them back. That way your accumulation of money is always growing in a continuous, unbroken pattern. It will always keep getting better. It cannot experience a reversal.

CHAPTER

THREE

LET'S TALK ABOUT TRADITIONAL FINANCIAL PLANNING

When it comes to your financial future, what do you see? More importantly, what do you not see? In life, most of the setbacks and lost opportunities we hear about in other people's lives, or experience in our own lives, are a result of what we do not see. To plan a financial future for ourselves, we must discover the things we do not see. We cannot keep doing the same things over and over and expect different results. That is the definition of insanity. Yet, for a large segment of our population, that is what is happening.

If you are an average Canadian, you are facing an enormous headwind that is keeping you from growing your personal economy efficiently. To create a sound financial future for yourself, here's what you need to see:

1) A foolproof easy-to-implement plan to address and solve the debt-financing issues most people are facing each and every day. Whether it is using the money in your plan to pay down your mortgage faster, or whether you should use it to pay cash when you buy your next

car or conjecturing the best way to financing life's other necessary or unexpected expenses, your money should be easily accessible. It would be far more valuable to you if you could simultaneously use these funds to accomplish all of the above, while your plan continues to churn along as though you never touched a loonie of it. This process will be described in the chapters that follow and can dramatically improve people's financial situation while lessening the burden of debt issues. The average Canadian is steeped in debt and the lending industry is having a heyday at your expense. Traditional financial planning is doing little to arrest—let alone reverse—the volume of interest that is stealing your early retirement.

2) More certainty in how your plan will provide a predictable retirement income that lasts as long as you do. It needs to be rock-solid and able to produce expected results without losing sleep, without the stomach-churning twists and turns, and without having to worry your investments might tank just when you're ready to retire. It would be brain-dead simple and pretty much able to operate on autopilot and not require a financing degree to implement. I'm guessing you are already busy enough and have no interest in spending your leisure time analyzing stock charts or surfing the internet for the perfect real estate investment (Yellen, 4).

Traditional financial planning lacks certainty and focuses on risk. You are continually asked, "What is your risk tolerance?" or "What is your risk profile?" It is an important question, since much of the risk when investing in mutual funds, or other securities, is passed on to you, not them – while *control* is passed on to them. The fund managers get paid a percentage of your money regardless of how well they manage it. Whether the stock market goes up or down, they get paid, as does the advisor. No matter what happens to your money, you are the only one taking any risk! And with little, or no control. If the market crashes, you lose money, AND you are the only one out of the group who is not getting paid. Whose money is it anyway?

Traditional planning vehicles are also fraught with tax and regulatory restrictions. They provide few options for using these funds in the ways we see fit. There are restricted withdrawals, and there are forced withdrawals with Canada Revenue Agency (CRA) waiting for the windfall. Furthermore, instead of being multipurposed, these vehicles lose their efficiency by having just one purpose. Who's in command here?

As Leonard A. Renier states:

> You would think it would be the goal of every financial advisor to achieve financial certainty for their clients. But they have been trained to sell different levels of risk instead.... That's because if financial companies offered certainty in your future, their company would be assuming all the risk and they are not in that business. So, without certainty, how would you describe your financial future? With the right conversations it may be possible to create certainty in your future. Wealthy people have been doing this for over a hundred years, but many financial companies find it very risky and *not* profitable to provide certainty" (Renier, 2018, 7).

Overall then, traditional financial planning is largely lacking in leverage, simplicity, control and certainty. These four hoped-for elements are nowhere to be found in today's traditional planning. So, is it time to step away from some of the traditional financial thinking and embrace a new perspective—one that offers you more control over your financial future?

Nelson Nash (2000, 43) says it best: "It never dawns on the financial gurus that you can control the financial environment in which you operate. Perhaps it is caused by lack of imagination, but whatever the cause, learning to control it is the most *profitable* thing you can do in a lifetime."

DEFINING WHAT YOU WANT

We would all like to take control of our financial environment and achieve financial freedom at some point in our lives. But what does financial freedom mean to you? If you could finally break the seemingly unending cycle of selling your time for money, what would you do with that time?

It is important to set purposeful goals, even in retirement. Nature abhors a vacuum. We humans cannot just exist and expect any enjoyment from that. Our free time must be filled with meaning and freshness. We can't be aimlessly loafing and remained intrigued for long. Growth, at any stage, pleases us. What are the activities that when we are engaged in cause the hours to fly by? Would you travel more? Take up a hobby? Work on your golf game? Start cycling to improve your health? Spend more time reading or volunteering? Enjoy more time with grandkids?

Unfortunately, very few people are on a path that will get them anywhere close to that kind of financial freedom. The vast majority of Canadians are on a trajectory to living a seriously diminished lifestyle in their old age, or at best, to having to continue working far longer than they would have anticipated.

CHAPTER

FOUR

WE ALL NEED A PLACE TO STORE MONEY

To begin, we need a place to store our cash. Everyone needs to put it somewhere—*before* it can be used elsewhere. Right now you probably use a chequing or savings account. From there, where does it go? Well, if your household is like most people's, it goes to pay for all kinds of everyday expenses: mortgage, food costs, utilities, insurance, cell phone, internet, car loans, etc. Then, it is gone!

So, is it fair to say that when you spend one dollar, it does *one thing* for you? It buys food. Or, it pays your cell phone bill. Maybe it goes to buy gas. And, once it is used for that one thing, it is GONE! It is a wealth transfer away from you and it can do nothing else for you.

But what if there was a way to have that one dollar *do more than one job for you?* What if that same dollar could do three or more jobs? What if it could do three or more jobs simply by adding *one* step to what you are already doing?

If I said to you, I have one dollar in this hand and three dollars in my other hand, which hand would you choose? Of course, you would always choose the hand with three dollars! But, if you are like most Canadians, you are *unknowingly choosing the one-dollar hand*; and the reason for this is because *no one has presented you the three-dollar hand*.

Well, I am going to present you the three-dollar hand! I want to help you understand there is a simple and effective process for reducing and/or eliminating wealth transfers that keep most Canadians stuck in a type of *financial bondage* year after year, and for many people, the rest of their lives. You no longer need to worry about these wealth transfers moving money *away* from you and out of your control every day. You do not have to rely on financial advisors who are either unaware of, or do not understand, the process for breaking this cycle other than to tell you that you must change your lifestyle and live with less; or rely on advisors who do not have access to the tools and products to reverse these transfers; or on advisors who simply choose not to go there because this process is not in their "job description." I will show you there's a better way!

As you will see, the **Infinite Banking Concept (IBC),** originated by R. Nelson Nash, is a practical and highly efficient way to store your cash, pay off debt, and save for retirement—all in a tax-free environment. And, the good news is IBC is available to everyone, not just business owners and the wealthy!

Simply put, using IBC means you save up a pool of cash that you own and control, borrow against that pool of cash (instead of from the bank), and pay for the things you were going to pay for anyway (such as paying down your mortgage, buying a car or piece of equipment, taking a holiday, etc.), then repay your pool of cash the same monthly payment, including interest, you would have *otherwise paid to a bank*. (As you can see, part of the "magic" of IBC is simply that it encourages us to *save up* before making purchases rather than buying things by going into debt) (Lara, Murphy, 2010, 206).

IBC is a way to put the banking function back at the you and me level where it really belongs. Think about that for a moment. If you could, in some way, repay your pool of cash all the interest you are currently paying (and *will* pay) to a bank or other lending institution, how much money would that be? It would include the interest on all your cars loans and *future* car loans. It would include the interest on your business loans, student loans, lines of credit, and even mortgages.

KEEPING UP WITH APPEARANCES

When we drive around our neighborhood, or any neighborhood, and see expensive vehicles parked in the driveway of a classy-looking home, we automatically think these people are doing well. The house is well kept, the lawn is maintained, trees beautifully adorn the property. It is a lovely sight. Alongside the home there might even be a motorhome and a boat. We automatically think these people are doing very well.

In *Becoming Your Own Banker*, Nash dedicates a chapter to Parkinson's Law. You may have heard of C. Northcote Parkinson, who wrote a little book called *Parkinson's Law*. In it, Parkinson brilliantly isolates some of the limitations of us all, particularly as they pertain to people's behaviour within a group. One thing he notes of people is that "a luxury, once enjoyed, becomes a necessity" (Nash, 2000, 28). Can you remember having a flip phone instead of the one you have today? Would you ever think of going back to having a cell phone that only worked as a phone? Me neither!

He also observed "expenses rise to equal income." When we get a pay raise it is quickly absorbed by a new definition of necessities! Our holidays become more luxurious, as do our automobile and restaurant choices.

So, you are driving down this neighborhood with the manicured lawns and nice cars in the driveway and you think, "They're doing really well." But in all likelihood these people are not much different than you or anyone else. They still have the same financial concerns as the rest of us. The only difference may be that their debts are larger because their income is high enough to support the payments. But, in many ways their concerns are the same. They wish they did not owe as much as they do, and they are hoping the rates do not go sky high when their mortgage renews. They are probably wondering if they will have enough money for retirement, just like everyone else, too. We are talking a huge chunk of our population here.

"Expenses rise to equal income." Today, almost anyone can have nice things. The question is how much is paid for and how much is owing? It is usually in the same proportion as everyone else. We tend to think, "If everyone else is doing it, then I am safe."

But paying interest to the bank is analogous to filling a 5-gallon bucket with water at a summer campground. You walk over to the well and start pumping the handle to fill your bucket. It does not take much effort to fill the bucket one pump at a time. The water flows easily and before you know it the bucket is filled.

Now, imagine the bucket has different sized holes in it: one for the motorhome, one for the boat, another for the luxury vehicle and a big one for the mortgage! How fast would you need to be pumping the handle to fill the bucket now? And, once you do get it filled, how much effort would be required to keep it filled, as the water continues pouring out the holes? Now you are getting tired and need a rest. What do you do? "In my kingdom," the Red Queen tells Alice in Wonderland, "you have to run as fast as you can to stay in the same place."

This is how vast numbers of Canadians are living today. The money must keep coming in incredibly fast to keep pace with the money that is leaking out. Unfortunately, for many, the money is leaking out faster than it is being pumped in, so the debts keep rising.

ARE YOU DOING WHAT EVERYONE ELSE IS DOING?

Are you financially stuck or do you have everything handled? If you are stuck, or think you could be doing better financially, does this have anything to do with paying interest to others, or because you are losing interest to yourself? Or, is it both?

You must ask ourselves some tough questions:

1.   Over the next years, if you keep doing what you have done over the *last* 5 years, where will you be in 5 years? In 10 years? In 20 years?
2.   If you are getting the majority of your financial advice from institutions that profit from lending money (ie., banks), is this to *your* advantage?
3.   Do you know how many dollars in interest you are paying to banks and lending institutions for the things you are financing compared to the initial cost of those purchases? In other words, what is the *volume* of interest?
4.   If only a minority of people are wealthy, do you want to follow what the majority of people do?
5.   What are you doing that is different from what everyone else is doing?
6.   Are you becoming more financially fit through the books you are reading or the podcasts you are listening to?
7.   Are you willing to read this book, and others like it, to understand the concept of how to become your own bank (your own source of financing) and take back control of your financial environment?
8.   If you could use IBC to get out of the debt cycle without changing your lifestyle, and save for your retirement at the same time, would it be worth learning about IBC?
9.   Where would you like to take your family on a holiday next year?
10. How much debt would you like to pay off in the next 3 years?

Do you have a financial plan that you know will help you succeed? Or, are you planning to fail by failing to plan? The truth is, without a plan you are like a ship without a rudder letting the currents and the headwinds toss you about, never knowing where you will end up.

With that in mind, consider the following:

1.   Would you like to use the money you are saving toward your retirement to also pay down your outstanding debt load?

2. Have you been shown how you can do your own financing for the next car you purchase *and* recapture all your lost-opportunity costs?
3. If you are a business owner, do you know how you can finance your next big equipment purchase or expansion and keep the money flowing inside your system?
4. Would you like to earn uninterrupted compounded growth on your money while using it elsewhere?
5. Are you getting at least three uses out of every dollar you earn?

 **CHAPTER**

FIVE

RECOVER EVERY LOONIE YOU PAY FOR YOUR NEXT CAR

Is it possible to spend and still grow your money? Well, let's look at buying a car, for example. We all do it, and seemingly we will continue to do it for the rest of our lives. If you do it the way most people do—by financing or even by paying cash—you may be shocked by how much wealth you are giving up and by not using IBC to buy your car.

Buckle up because I am about to reveal all the details of how IBC works and how it will forever change the way you think about money and financing. Many of the ideas presented in this chapter are inspired from Pamela Yellen's *Bank On Yourself* (2009). She has done a superb job of putting car buying, and financing in general, into perspective.

Frequently, when I am sitting with potential clients and going through this process they shake their heads in disbelief and say, *it's too good to be true*. I will admit when I first stumbled across the concept, I, too, thought the same thing. I was even more surprised to discover that hundreds of thousands of people had been doing their financing this way for decades. Why did not I know about this?

Okay, let's assume that over the next 40 years you will need to buy a new car every 4 years. Using car purchases is a great example since we all can relate to this process. Any potential pain we may incur with this new expense is usually offset by the grand feeling of having a new set of wheels under us as we drive around. The pleasing smell, the newness, the elegant style, the handling, the cleanliness, and the greater number of options we have with this new vehicle has its benefits, even if it was a pre-owned vehicle you bought on Kijiji.

But what if you could get back every nickel you paid for the car, along with any interest you would have paid to banks or other lenders? This is a serious question. Are you also starting to think it sounds *too good to be true?* If it were true, what impact would that make on your personal economic balance? I am guessing you would take more holidays, or at least more luxurious holidays, without the guilt, because you know you are going to recover whatever you spend.

In fact, with all the money you would save over a 30- or 40-year period, there is no reason you would not retire with that much more money to play with.

To understand the process, let's jump in the driver's seat and look at the most common ways people finance and purchase cars.

FINANCING CARS USING OTHER PEOPLE'S MONEY

Let's say you decide to buy a new car. You are sitting at the dealership signing the paperwork. The settling cost of the car is $35,000. Finally, it is "yours."

The sales team helps you come up with a financing arrangement with a lender that suits your budget. The lender will charge you 6% interest and your monthly payments will be $819.35 per month over the next 48 months. That means over the next four years the car will cost you $39,328.

Now, let's skip ahead. Four years have passed and you have a four-year-old car worth whatever its trade in value is. You have said goodbye forever to $39,328.

But who has your $39,328? The lender, of course, has your money because it was *theirs* to start with. They paid the car company for your car exactly four years earlier and you paid them back over time.

Now it is time to purchase another car. Okay, so you use its trade-in value and you decide to borrow another $35,000.

Where did the lender get the money they are going to lend you? Any guesses? As Pamela Yellen (2009), author of *Bank on Yourself* reminds us, they got it from *you!* They also got it from others like you who do not practice the IBC way of financing cars.

If you play this out over 40 years, financing just *one* car at a time this way (totaling 10 cars) will cost you $393,280! But, if you are like most people and have two or more cars in your driveway, then you can see the wealth transfer away from you could be twice that much, or even more.

Will you ever see a Canadian loonie of that money again? I am afraid not. Are you ever going to earn compound interest on a dollar of that money? *You never will.* This is what happens when you let someone else control the financing function in your life. Everyone (the lender, the dealership, and the car company) is making money on these transactions. But, not you!

This is how traditional financing works and it seems most people, those who have not yet discovered IBC, are okay with it. Pamela Yellen says many people could comfortably retire on the money they could recapture just by paying for their cars and vacations this way (2009, 18). It is quite likely that far more of your hard-earned income will go to financing cars in your lifetime than will ever go toward your retirement. Think about it.

Are you putting as much money away toward your retirement as you are putting into buying the vehicles that you own? Many people are and many, mostly younger people, are not. Perhaps best of all, using IBC allows you to grow you nest egg at the same time you pay for vehicles—predictably so. That way you don't lose any sleep over it.

LEASING CARS

What about leasing your car? Leasing has become popular for one reason: the monthly payments are lower. But, leasing is the costliest option. After the lease is up you have nothing to show for it, and all your money is in the hands of someone else. There is no use talking about leasing your cars unless you are leasing them to yourself using your own IBC plan to do it with.

If you are a business owner, the business pays monthly leasing costs to the IBC plan that you own personally. It becomes a deductible business expense to the business and a small profit center for you. You get to drive the vehicle and act as leaser to your business.

PAYING CASH FOR CARS

Perhaps you are thinking that paying cash is a better solution than financing or leasing. But is paying cash not just another form of financing? Nelson Nash points out, "You finance everything you buy. When you borrow you pay interest to someone else. When you pay cash, you give up the interest you could have earned otherwise."

Either way, you are giving up interest. You are either paying interest or you are passing up interest. All You have done is proven to yourself that you have the ability to save and that you can delay gratification. But, the moment you withdraw it from savings is the moment it stops working for you. You get no further uses from it.

You may be thinking what is being taught here is not that applicable to you. I assure you, it is very applicable. Before I explain, I want you to understand that I get where you are coming from. Before I understood the power and the benefits of IBC I was exactly where you are. After all, I was once a Dave Ramsey fan: "Get out of debt. Learn to pay cash for everything." Even, "Cut up your credit cards. Think of all the interest payments we could save."

It is true that we were not *paying* interest to a lender when we withdraw our own money to pay cash, but we were not *earning* money on our cash either, which should be our bigger concern. With this type of transaction our money had *one* use and it was gone! It was now earning interest for someone else, perhaps the sellers or the financiers of the car. If we thought like a bank, we would lend our own money to ourselves so we could earn interest on it non-stop. So, why would you and I not do that?

Perhaps you are thinking, "Why don't I just use a savings account at my local bank and use that money to buy the car?" Here is the problem. If you have a savings account at the bank, how much interest are you earning on it? Probably not very much. As I write this today a 5-year GIC is paying 1.42% annually. Let's say it's earning 3%. Is it taxable? Yes. So, what you are earning is even *less*. Not only that, is it locked in for the five years? Yes. So, a GIC is not a good savings vehicle for liquidity and accessibility, which is what is needed for this purpose. If you leave it in and request a loan from the bank is that a hassle? Yes. Is there a credit check? Yes. Is a credit check damaging? Yes. Where does the interest for the loan you are paying go? To the bank.

Even if the money was accessible and you *withdrew* the money, so you could pay cash, would that be a good option? No. Why? Because your funds are depleted. You are earning ZERO! So, now you must start building up that account again and the interest you are earning is miniscule until the principle gets built back up.

With this low-interest-rate environment, it is no wonder people do not put more value on the money they have. People who understand the IBC strategy do not think this way.

We understand the powerful long-term effects of earning uninterrupted compounded growth on our money in a tax-exempt environment. Whatever amount we borrow, that same amount continues to earn interest and dividends for as long as we live and as long as our IBC plan is in force. As you will see shortly, now it is working for us instead of against us. But if you pay cash by *withdrawing* your money each time you buy a car you are essentially now transferring it to someone else, so it can compound for them.

HOW WE PREVIOUSLY BOUGHT CARS

Before I tell you how to buy your next car using the IBC method, I want to tell you how my wife Sue, and I used to buy cars. We would save and save and after a few years have enough money in our bank account for a reasonably nice car. In the meantime, we would delay gratification, skip going out to dinner, and generally cut back on our lifestyle.

When the time came, we would shop around on Kijiji, or pop into dealerships, and generally get excited about what kind of car we would buy. We knew what colour, make and model, and what options we wanted. We always had fun looking for cars to buy, and still do today. There is probably a reason for that. I remember on our first date, after a nice, quiet Sunday night dinner at Edmonton's High Level Café, I said to Sue, "Hey I'm looking at buying a nicer car. Do you want to cruise around to the dealerships and look for cars with me?"

To my delight, she accepted, so she must have thought, "How romantic and fun this sounds." The dealerships were all closed so we had them to ourselves. We walked around and had great discussions on what wheels to buy. I was impressed by how much she knew about cars. It was a memorable night.

But when I was ready to buy, I withdrew money from my savings account and line of credit, and paid cash for my new vehicle. I continued to follow that same process in the years that followed, sometimes paying cash, sometimes with a line of credit, and sometimes leasing. By doing so, I continued to send my money to others and never saw it again.

As I said earlier, paying cash for our cars was still *financing* them since we were now *giving up* interest. So, we were not taking advantage of the "eighth wonder of the world" (compound interest). That means it was costing us the potential earnings we could have made from those dollars had we invested them. *So really, we were financing the losses of what we could have been earning on our money.* In financial lingo we call that lost-opportunity cost. It was a wealth transfer away from us that we will never see again. We got the car, but not the money. This is how we have all been taught to buy our cars.

Each time we make a cash payment, it ends up back in someone's bank account—the one who is financing everything! And what do they do with it? You guessed it; they lend it out again. Isn't that what we should be doing?

Sue and I were still dating several months later, and I asked her if she would like to go house shopping with me. To my delight, she accepted, so she must have thought, "How romantic and fun this sounds." I was impressed by how much she knew about houses. We finally picked out the house that best suited ... *her.* I saw she was *committed* to that house and thought to myself *it would be a great house for us to begin our lives together in.* She had more money than I had and helped with the down payment. You can guess the rest of the story. Not long after, I asked Sue to marry me… and, *it was a great house for us to begin our lives together in!* It was the smartest purchase I've ever made.

As mentioned before, banking is all about accumulating money and making loans to people who will pay them back. Rather than pay the bank, why not pay ourselves? If we make loans to ourselves—and pay them back—our money keeps growing in a continuous unbroken pattern, while we enjoy the things we want. And, on top of that, when using an IBC plan, your money cannot experience a reversal. No more uncertainty!

THINKING LIKE A BANKER - BUYING A CAR THE IBC WAY

So, now let's look at the IBC way of buying your next car when you start thinking like a banker and observe how much faster your wealth will grow. Instead of borrowing the $35,000 from the financing company, you borrow against the money in your IBC plan, which has been properly set up for quick cash value growth. You receive the $35,000 from your IBC plan, which has now been directly deposited into your chequing account and pay the dealership directly for the full value of the car. (For now, do not get hung up on how to get $35,000 into your IBC plan. There are several ways to do it, as you will see in the next chapter).

So now, instead of your monthly payments going to a financing company, you set up preauthorized payments to your IBC plan to replenish your pool of money you borrowed against. You are making payments just like you would to a finance company, but the money is going back into *your* own system. You are taking your money from one of your pockets and putting it in another one of your pockets. Isn't that better than putting it into someone else's pocket? And, you have now *Become Your Own Source of Financing* (which is also the title of my previous book).

Let's look ahead now. Four years have gone by and you have paid off your loan to yourself. Every nickel you borrowed is now available to you to borrow again. You have recaptured the cost of your car in full. You ended up with the car and all the money you paid for the car! It gets even better than that. You will likely have *more* money than what you paid back to your plan!

One of the hallmarks of the IBC plan is that your money continues to grow even if you've borrowed it for something else. For that entire four years, the full $35,000 you used to pay off the car continued to earn money inside your IBC plan. It is as though you had not touched a loonie of it. Yes, you heard right! Your IBC plan will continue to grow earning interest and dividends on the full amount even when you use that money for something else!

You can reuse your IBC money as many times as you want for any type of purchase, since every dollar you repay on your IBC loan is money you can immediately use again.

So, by buying all your cars this way, the money that would have gone out the door and into someone else's hands stays with you. Instead of using a bank or a finance company, *you* are performing the banking function in your life—with a pool of money *you* own and control. And, of course, every one of the dollars you pay back can be borrowed again and again and again. If you do this for every car you purchase over the next 40 years, you will have in your possession, the $393,280 the finance company, dealership and car manufacturer would have made off you!

You are cutting out the middle person and changing the direction your money is flowing. Money that was flowing away from you and into someone else's hands is now flowing back to you. It is your money and it has been working for you, compounding over a span of 40 years!

That's what makes this approach superior to even paying cash. Once you pay cash, by *withdrawing* your money, it's gone. You can no longer make compound interest on that money. It's not yours anymore! With the IBC plan, you never have to give up the compounding effect because you are not *withdrawing* the money and thus giving up its earning potential. Instead, you are keeping the money and *borrowing* against it, at a small cost, and letting it continue to grow. That's what makes thinking like a banker and using the IBC plan the most efficient system there is for financing what matters to you.

So, what do you think now? How much faster do you think your wealth will grow if you change the direction your money is flowing, and all your financing payments end up replenishing what you have access to in your own wealth pool?

Consider your mortgage. If you reverse your mortgage payments of say $2,000 or $3,500 per month so they are now coming toward you, how much sooner could you retire?

The same process can be used to get back the money from any major purchase you make in life, including a dream vacation, equipment purchases, university costs, a second home somewhere warm that you have been dreaming about, or just to retire on that much sooner. There are an infinite number of ways IBC can be used, hence the name *Infinite Banking Concept!*

CHAPTER
SIX

BANKING AND LIFE INSURANCE

I have heard Nelson Nash give many talks, whether at the annual Nelson Nash Institute Think Tank in Birmingham, Alabama or closer to home in Kelowna, BC. I'm always amazed by his passion, intelligence and conviction. When Nelson stands up and starts a seminar, it usually begins with something like this: "The whole idea is to recapture the interest that one is paying to banks and finance companies for the major items we need during a lifetime, such as automobiles, major appliances, education, homes, investment opportunities, business equipment, etc."

Though banking has been around since biblical times and life insurance has been around longer than automobiles, Nelson saw that both could be used together by anyone, not just the wealthy or business owners. He discovered that by running your dollars through a specially designed dividend-paying-life-insurance policy and maximum-funding it, you can create your own source of financing and become your own bank. And in doing so, you can recover all your borrowing costs and accelerate your wealth significantly faster. Your capital continues to grow, even while you borrow against it, thus solving the problem of lost-opportunity costs on your spending and savings.

This, he discovered, could be done *without* changing your cash flow or reducing your lifestyle. Rather, it is simply by redirecting those same dollars that you use to pay your everyday expenses and flowing them through your life insurance policy first, *before* they are used for your everyday living expenses. This pool of money can be used to pay down debts, make purchases, and take advantage of financial opportunities. By borrowing against your pool of money and financing your purchases with it, the payments that would have otherwise gone to a bank, or financing company, are paid back to your own private monetary system. This results in more money flowing into your system, with each dollar performing multiple uses.

A HAND UP WITH IBC

To see a practical example of how to create your own source of financing and thinking like a banker, here is a fictionalized account of a typical conversation I would have with a married couple who find themselves facing a headwind of debt and the reduced level of freedom that comes along with it. This couple sees a massive amount of their income going out the door each month to service both their debt and their other monthly expenses—a situation that is all too common in the world we live in today. This financial drain is the number one concern they have. It is also a concern that is largely overlooked and never seems to be addressed in the mainstream financial-planning world.

Jason and Joelle (not their real names) have been married for 13 years. They have two kids they adore, ages 11 and 9. Jason is a master electrician with his own contracting company and Joelle is an accountant with her own practice. Together they have a good income. In two previous meetings, I have conducted a "fact-find" with them and now have a picture of their current personal economy. As is more common than not, they are using a high percentage of their income to pay interest to financing companies. We have talked about how they have been conditioned, by well-meaning people, to think about money and how this thinking has led them to the financial situation they are now facing. That is, if they keep doing what they are doing, it will take them decades to get out of debt. For the most part, they have done everything right. They are not living above their means. In fact, they are managing their affairs better than most people.

What has been holding them back is their conditioned thinking. As mentioned before, conditioned thinking is like a rut and it takes perseverance to get out of that rut. Think about how your vehicle reacts when driving in a rut. It is hard to get out of it, and it may take you several tries before you finally succeed. Once out, you may have to alter your route to find another road to your destination: one that is smooth— perhaps the road less travelled. The IBC road.

Jason and Joelle would like to find a better way to get the banks off their backs and pay off their mortgage sooner. They have been told they can pay down their mortgage faster with a lump sum payment once a year, but that has never panned out. Besides, they may need that money for an emergency if one of their parents dies or if the roof starts to leak. The rut they are in is that they have been conditioned to think they need banks to purchase the things they need in life. So, without question they continue sending wads of money to these institutions knowing they will never see a nickel of it again.

Furthermore, they are conditioned to feel *guilt-ridden* if they do not listen to others who are telling them to go without, to save up, to not spend, to pay cash, and to risk their money in the stock market, because that is what everyone else is doing. Rut thinking does not challenge the status quo or question whether something is good or bad, it just directs people to "go with the flow."

Jason and Joelle are not looking for a handout, but a hand up. They do not yet realize that by adding *one simple step* to how they were taught to think about money they can begin getting *three uses out of every dollar*. Today they are getting only one use—and then it's gone!

I borrowed the concept of "three uses of every dollar" from a highly respected friend and colleague of mine, Chris Bay, of Lawrence, Kansas. Chris works together with Mike Everett and early in 2018 I joined them for the "boot camp" they offer their clients. I owe them both a huge debt of gratitude, since whenever I explain IBC using their "three uses of every dollar" concept, my clients immediately get it! Here's how it goes:

THREE USES OF EVERY DOLLAR

Me: If I said to you, I have one dollar in this hand and three dollars in the other hand, which hand would you choose?

Joelle: The three-dollar hand.

Me: Of course. Who wouldn't? So, now I'm going to show you how to pick that better hand in real life: how to get *three uses* out of every dollar.

Jason: Okay …

Me: When you get paid, where does your money get deposited?

Joelle: The bank?

Me: Yes. Banks are smart enough to make that happen by direct deposit, right? What happens to it after it's deposited?

Joelle: It goes to pay for all our expenses, like our mortgage, food, utilities, car loans, car insurance, house insurance, life insurance.

Me: Anything else?

Jason: Gas, cell phone, line of credit, credit card, internet, and all the other living expenses.

Me: It's a lot, isn't it? You said you have life insurance?

Jason: Yes. We have term insurance on both of us.

Me: Okay, and are you investing any money? Are you putting away money for retirement? Are these any of your goals?

Joelle: Yes, we have RRSPs and we're trying to put away 5% of each of our incomes.

Me: Would you like to be doing more?

Joelle: We would, but it seems like our mortgage payments, car loans, and all these expenses are killing us.

Me: Well, let's look at your monthly expenses. For simplicity sake, let's say you have just *one dollar* that covers all those expenses… like your mortgage, food, utilities, car loans, car insurance, house insurance, life insurance, RRSP, gas, cell phone, line of credit, credit card, internet, and on and on. That's really stretching that dollar, isn't it?

Jason: Definitely.

Me: So that ONE dollar goes to your bank and it gets divided up among *ALL* your expenses. Right now, when you spend one dollar, it does *one* thing for you. It buys food or it buys gas. Maybe it pays the utility bill. But once it leaves your hands, it's GONE. It can do nothing else.

            What I'm going to show you is how to get **three uses out of every dollar** simply by adding ONE step to the process.

            All you have to do is make one little change to your cash flow. Every month when your income gets deposited into the bank, instead of it *all* going immediately to your expenses, as we are all taught to do, we are going to simply change the direction it goes and have some of it deposited into your own "private banking system." This is your "bank", but not the bricks and mortar kind, and it is not even a bank. It is where you store money. It's your "warehouse of wealth."

Jason: How is that possible?

Me: Using a process conceived in the mind of Nelson Nash, your own private banking system is created using what he calls an "Infinite Banking Concept" (IBC) policy. The IBC policy is a participating dividend-paying-life-insurance policy. You put money into an IBC policy through what we call *premium deposits*.

Most people think of life insurance deposits as an *expense*, right? That's true if your life insurance is *term* life insurance which has no cash value. But, that's not the case here. This is your private financing pool-of-wealth inside an IBC policy. Remember, IBC is the strategy and it must be implemented on a tangible platform. Participating dividend-paying life insurance is the perfect platform.

So, if this is your own powerful private financing system, would you want your deposits to be small or large?

Jason: Large, of course!

Me: Yes, the larger the better because you own and control it. Also, when you send money into your IBC life insurance policy, what else do you get?

Joelle: Life insurance! We get a death benefit!

Me: Exactly! You get life insurance! That's *one* use you get out of every dollar you send to your IBC policy. So, if you are getting a life insurance death benefit with your IBC policy, do you need to keep sending money every month over to your *expense* side, to pay for your term life insurance?

Joelle: Ha! No, I guess not.

Me: That's right! So, **one** of the uses of every dollar deposited on the IBC side is that it provides a life insurance *death benefit* that grows every month. Not only are you getting the death benefit here on the IBC side, you are *eliminating* the term insurance payments on the *expense* side.

Joelle: So, let me see if I have this right. On the IBC side, we have permanent life insurance, which gives us increased protection every year. That's awesome! I didn't want us to ever lose our life insurance when we got older, but I didn't think we'd have a choice. The term insurance we have now renews when we're 48, and then it gets so expensive that we were planning to drop it. Get this: it goes from costing us $120 per month to over $900 per month! That's insane!

Me: Ha-ha! Term insurance protects you when you are young, which is great. But people drop it at renewal, when it gets too expensive. Because of this, only 1% of term insurance is ever paid out as a claim. So, 99% of the time, it's money you spend and will never see again. That's not true of an IBC policy. Most people want life insurance when they get older and an IBC policy lasts as long as you do. It will pay out no matter how old you are. And, that's only **one** use of your dollar.

A **second** use of your dollar is *uninterrupted savings*. What this means is that the "eighth wonder of the world"— compounded growth—is *never* interrupted. And, it grows tax exempt! So, if you're getting compounded growth on the *IBC* side, would you need to keep sending as much money to your retirement fund over on the *expense* side?

Jason: No, we wouldn't! Wow! That takes a big load off my mind because we were getting worried about having all our "retirement eggs" in the mutual fund basket.

Me: Exactly! Now, the *third* use of every dollar, which I get most excited about, is *financing!* We can use these dollars anywhere, anytime, because we can take loans *against* our policy. We can now take those dollars, put them right back into our bank account and use them for *expenses or to pay down debt*. This creates *cash flow*.

Here is the cycle: We borrow against our cash value. We use that money to pay down *outside* debt. We call outside debt a *headwind*, as Nelson Nash says. We repay our loan to our own IBC system, *plus interest*. We call that *inside* debt. Inside debt can work to our advantage. All the while, our cash value is compounding, uninterrupted, tax-free inside our policy.

Joelle: What you're saying, is that it's the same dollar we were spending before on the expense side, but it now gets us 3 uses:

1) a death benefit,

2) uninterrupted compound growth, and

3) financing.

So, that means we can use those borrowed dollars from our IBC policy to pay down our debt on the expense side, then pay back the money, plus interest to the insurance company. But, during that whole time our money is still compounding on 100% of our dollars?

Me: You nailed it!

Jason: That's not how we were taught to think about money. We were taught that once you pay for something, that money's gone. Now you're telling us we can run those dollars through our "private financing system" first, then pay our expenses and get three uses out of every dollar we earn.

Me: Yes, and we can even take it a step further. Let's say you have over $30,000 in your cash value, and you want to use that to buy your next car. Instead of borrowing from a bank, you take a *policy loan* for $30,000. Instead of paying a bank back, you're paying your system back for the loan.

Joelle: If we're borrowing from a bank, we'll never see those dollars again. But here, we're putting those dollars back where we can use them again, right?

Me: You got it.

Jason: We have two cars that we replace every four years. Over the next 40 years that's 20 cars times $30,000. That's $600,000 that we would pay back to our system! I get it!! Otherwise, if we keep doing what we've been doing, our money will keep going to the bank's coffers.

Me: And this way, your cash value is still compounding inside your policy and generating more dollars.

Jason: This could certainly fast-track our retirement savings into high gear. Let's get our act in gear, honey!

Joelle: But, isn't there an interest cost for that money we borrow?

Me: Yes, the life insurance company charges you interest for any outstanding policy loan, since they are lending you the money from the same account that is paying you the dividend. *Your* money, however, is still in your policy as though you never touched a loonie of it. This can offset the cost of borrowing it. You stand to make *more* money inside your policy than the insurance company is charging you for borrowing it. If you *withdrew* the money, you would stop its growth. But instead, you're taking a *loan* against your cash value.

Jason: So, *borrow*, don't withdraw.

Me: Right. And, when you get around to paying it back, pay yourself at least what the insurance company is charging you. I charge myself 10%, and many of our clients choose to do the same. Remember, every dollar you pay back is a dollar you can borrow again. Now you're thinking like a bank and reusing your money.

Jason: Like the banks do.

Joelle: It's true, Jason. What do the banks do as soon as they get deposits? They lend it out! That's what we would be doing for ourselves. Lending it out to ourselves for the things we need in life. Just like the banks do.

Jason: What if we did what my parents do every time they buy a car and just *withdraw* money from their high interest savings account and pay cash? Would this be better than *borrowing* from our IBC policy?

Me: Well, when they *withdraw* the money from their bank account and pay cash, what are they giving up?

Joelle: Compounded growth! They are stopping the "eighth wonder of the world"!

Me: Exactly! They are stopping their money from working. They got one use out of their money and it is gone!

           Well, are you ready to get started?

Joelle: Yes. Thank you! This is what we've been looking for our entire lives—a way to beat the banks at their own game!

Jason: I agree. The sooner, the better.

End of discussion

The above scenario is meant to illustrate how the Infinite Banking Concept can be used in an everyday situation. Whenever a situation, such as the one with Jason and Joelle plays out, a lot of pre-teaching and education on their part has gone on prior to the meeting. Most likely they have read Nash's *Becoming Your Own Banker,* or listened to the CD of that book, or they have been at a presentation offered by me or another IBC Practitioner.

DIVIDENDS

To understand where insurance-policy dividends come from a brief explanation is necessary. When designing life insurance policies, the rate makers factor in the analyses done by actuaries, such as how long a large group of selected healthy people (who were healthy enough to qualify for life insurance) will live. The rate makers will also factor in interest earnings on the premium deposits paid by policy owners, the number and value of death claims expected over a specified time frame, and the expected cost of administration. If the rate makers get it right (and they are extremely accurate), the company makes a profit and you receive a dividend.

If the company does not make a profit, you will not receive a dividend. This is rarely, if ever, the case. The handful of insurers we use have declared dividends each year for well over 100 consecutive years. Once a dividend is declared its value is guaranteed from that point on. Unlike securities, and universal life policies, the policy can never lose value.

As Nash (2000, 23) correctly states, "The word dividend was used by the insurance industry to describe this dispersal and it stuck with us, but the correct classification is a *return of premium* … which is not a taxable event. … If the owner uses the dividend to purchase paid up additional insurance … the result is an ever-increasing tax-deferred accumulation of cash values that support an ever-increasing death benefit."

SOUNDS TOO GOOD TO BE TRUE

Like I said before, when I present this system to clients, I hear, "This sounds too good to be true." In other words, it sounds too easy. That's understandable. We feel guilty, thinking we should be doing something more to make this happen. I, too, was first shocked, then amazed to discover I could be using my money in one place to make a purchase, while still growing it somewhere else—and to come out financially ahead by doing so!

I grew up, like a lot of us did, learning nothing came about without hard work. Growing up on a beef and grain farm, my siblings and I would go to the barn to help our dad with chores *before* we could get ready for school. We hardly ever took holidays, and, for the most part, hard work seemed to never end. So, I can relate to people when they say, "It's too good to be true." It's like saying the chores will get done even if I sleep in. Most of us have had to struggle to get anything accomplished, so we don't think we should be entitled to having it so easy. We have been conditioned to think this way.

With IBC, the mechanics are already in place to "have our cake and eat it, too," as the saying goes. It's part of the package. We do not have to exert effort to have our cash value grow while we are using it elsewhere. That would be like feeling guilty while driving our car, as we sit so comfortably in our cushy leather seats, because the pistons are working so hard.

A NEEDS-BASED APPROACH

It should be noted that neither you, nor your advisor, should move ahead with a plan before conducting a "needs-based approach" to your situation. In all circumstances your advisor should make you aware that the product being discussed is life insurance. Life insurance is the platform that allows you the flexibility to reuse your dollars over and over again.

Specifically, it is a whole-life insurance policy with all the necessary additional riders to make the product most appealing and capable for this purpose. And you are required to make deposits over and above the cost of the insurance. In other words, it is maximum funded, up to the exempt test policy limits (ETP), requiring paid-up additions (PUA), which systematically increase the death benefit coverage each year, and also includes other riders to suit your specific needs, such as term insurance, critical illness, waiver of premium in case of disability, etc.

Structuring it in this unique way can add significantly more cash value at the end of the first year and ensuing years, than with a traditionally designed policy. Almost every dollar of any *excess deposit* goes directly to cash value, where it compounds, exempt from taxation, along with any dividends accredited. This, of course, is a highly attractive place to deposit cash. And, the death benefit increases in proportion to any excess deposits that buy paid-up additional insurance.

Exempt test policy limits, also known as the maximum tax actuarial reserve (MTAR) limits, are strictly enforced. While there is lots of room for tax-exempt growth inside a whole-life policy, contributions are restricted to ensure these policies are not viewed as tax havens. The issuing insurer takes responsibility for insuring policy holders do not exceed the limit. But the fact that there are restrictions ought to tell us something. These policies are so appealing the government has enforced limits on how much money we can deposit into them.

TAKING A CUT IN COMMISSION

When an IBC-type policy is issued, the advisor will take anywhere from a 40% to 80% cut in their commission. Their commission is determined mostly by the cost of insurance which may be only 20% to 60% of the premium deposit. Even though the premium deposits can be extremely large for an IBC policy, any extra money the client puts into the policy, over and above the insurance costs pays very little commission, and, as stated, is turned into accessible cash value for the client's use.

In fact, once your policy has been approved and you have qualified for the death benefit, you can access your available cash value within a matter of weeks after you make your deposit. The frequency of your premiums deposits (e.g., monthly or annually), will, of course, determine how much cash value is available to you. However, most policy holders build up their policy values, called the *start up phase*, over a minimum of a year or two, before taking loans against it.

Commissions for *traditional* life insurance policies are paid on 100% of the monthly or annual premium deposits. Not so with IBC structured policies. As mentioned, IBC practitioners will take a *40% to 80% pay cut* versus commissions paid when selling traditional insurance. The reaction you get when you tell traditional financial advisors this piece of information is mixed. I have talked with many non-IBC advisors about IBC, and right away, after hearing the commission details, start to protest. "What do you mean I have to cut my compensation?" End of discussion.

Why would advisors be willing to take a 40% to 80% cut in their commission? How could that be good for business? For one thing, as IBC practitioners, our clients are going to own many more plans than clients who are buying traditional plans. Our IBC clients see much more value in these policies and realize they can do more with their money when they run it through these plans before they purchase other things. As a result, they buy more policies, so compensation is not an issue for the advisor.

The IBC practitioner also receives more referrals, often without even asking for them, than other advisors. Clients spread the word because they see this as a way to recapture the lost-opportunity costs of almost every transaction they can make.

IMPORTANT NOTE: *We are not talking about a universal life (UL) policy, which is structured entirely differently than a whole-life (WL) policy. With UL, cash values are not fully accessible for 10 years and they may vary widely since they are usually based on stock market returns.* **The IBC concept will <u>not work</u> using a UL policy.**

CHAPTER
SEVEN

USING IBC AS INTENDED

Let's say you are the type of person who would like to:

- rapidly eliminate outside debt,
- finance your non-debt living expenses,
- have passive retirement income when the time comes,
- transfer your wealth tax-free at death.

Let's briefly explain how each of these wishes could become reality.

RAPIDLY ELIMINATE OUTSIDE DEBT

When eliminating debt, the behaviour of the policy owner is more important than the policy itself. It is the individual who makes it effective. Outside debt owing on credit cards, car loans, lines of credit, and even mortgages, can be paid off using the cash value of your policy if the cash value is sufficient. You can only borrow what is available and is yours to start with. When you take a policy loan to pay off a truck loan, for instance, you can redirect those payments back to your policy. Most likely, you will need to start additional policies, as more and more outside debt payments are redirected toward your "private banking system." Remember your cash value is still receiving dividends, and earning interest daily, inside your policy, compensating for the borrowing costs you are paying to the insurance company. As well, your repayments are building your policy back up and you can reuse this money all over again.

FINANCE YOUR NON-DEBT LIVING EXPENSES

After your debt is gone, IBC can be used to finance living expenses. We've all been taught to use our dollars to pay our bills. That's good. But when you spend one dollar, it does one thing for you. It buys groceries. It pays gas. It pays off your credit card balance each month. But once it leaves your hands, it is gone. It can do nothing else for you.

Wouldn't it make more sense to, every so often, use policy loans? What would stop you from taking two- or three-months worth of future anticipated credit card payments as a policy loan and using this to make your life run? Instead of getting one use and it's gone, now the money you borrowed will pay off your credit card AND it is still compounding for you while you are repaying the balance, thus, running the dollars through you own system that you control.

Remember, when you take a policy loan, you stand to gain if dollar for dollar the loan costs are less than the uninterrupted growth of your policy. It also may require starting multiple policies. Here, you become your own financing source to handle most of your expenses. At this point you are running every dollar you can through your system before you invest or spend a dollar—even for a night out! This way, your money is doing double duty. You could even extend your financing activities, and act as lender for your family, or business. You can discuss this option with your advisor, to determine if this is something that would benefit you when the time comes.

A FLEXIBLE TOOL FOR PASSIVE RETIREMENT INCOME

As you approach retirement, the growth in your policies are at their best, since it is these later years when your annual dividend allotments are the greatest! By then you could possibly have numerous policies with a million or two million dollars in cash value. Now you want the money. How do you get it?

Accessing the cash value of your policy for passive income during your golden years is an integral part of the planning strategy. There are three main ways to do this:

1. withdraw funds from the policy
2. take out a policy loan
3. collateral assignment – take out a loan from a "third party" financial institution using the policy as collateral

The first two methods will trigger taxation at some point. The third method, since it does not require *direct* access of your funds, does not trigger tax. (This is explained below under *Collateral Assignment*). The following explanation of adjusted cost base (ACB) explains how tax is calculated using the first two methods. It is not the purpose of this book for you to understand how ACB works at this point, other than that it determines taxation levels of policy loans, or withdrawals. (You can skip the explanation if you wish).

ADJUSTED COST BASE (ACB)

Basically, a policy's ACB is the sum total you paid in premium deposits less the sum total of the net cost of pure insurance (NCPI) deductions made to the policy. NCPI is the real cost of insurance per $1000 of death benefit for your age, so as you age the NCPI continues to increase. Luckily, this is of little concern to you since with a whole-life policy, your cost of insurance is guaranteed to stay the same for your whole life. It is however, a concern for the insurance company since the company must use the NCPI to calculate the ACB (There are several other factors that go into the calculation, but they are not pertinent to our discussion here).

When you take loans from your policies up to the ACB limit, the loans themselves are tax-free. Every time a policy loan is issued there is a dollar for dollar reduction in the ACB. When and if the ACB is reduced to zero, then further policy loans become *taxable*. This means the dollars you receive from a policy loan – from a policy with zero ACB – are included in your taxable income. The good news is you get a *tax deduction* every time you repay a policy loan that was taxable. Every dollar you add to the policy increases the ACB. Okay, enough of the technical stuff.

POLICY WITHDRAWALS

When you need retirement income, one option is to arrange monthly or annual withdrawals from your policy. However, there are a few factors to consider. First, these withdrawals are final, so they can never be repaid to your policy. Your policy's cash value and death benefit will therefore be reduced accordingly.

Second, all or part of the policy withdrawal may be taxable. Whenever the cash surrender value (CSV) of a policy exceeds its adjusted cost base (ACB), withdrawals will trigger taxation. For example, if 40% of the total CSV is comprised of non-taxable ACB, and 60% of the total CSV is taxable, then 40% of the withdrawal will be treated as non-taxable, while 60% of the withdrawal will be taxable. Ultimately, the ACB of the life insurance policy will reach zero and when that happens 100% of a withdrawal will be taxable. (Sun Life's, "An Advisor's Guide to Leveraging a Life Insurance Policy," 810-2876-07-17). So, what about policy loans during retirement.

POLICY LOANS

Policy loans can be used for retirement income, but these loans differ from the policy loans we use to buy our car or pay down our mortgage. Policy loans for retirement income are loans we may never pay back. If we set up our policy to pay us an income every year, each loan we take out on it reduces our policy's death benefit and interest is paid to the participating account for each new loan. That's the downside. The upside is that we are not giving up the earning potential of our policy's cash value since we have left it alone. It is still in the policy and we are taking a loan against it. The income we are receiving is coming from the participating account of the insurance company. Our policy will remain in force for as long as the earning potential of our cash value can exceed the interest costs for the growing number of loans we are taking for income. When it comes to this point we must stop taking policy loans in order to keep the life insurance coverage in force.

A policy loan is an advance against the death benefit, paid under the terms of the policy. So, while terms like "policy loan" and "borrow" are used to describe this method of accessing your cash, the legal requirements and obligations are different from when a person uses the policy as collateral for a loan or for a line of credit from a 'third party' financial institution.

Policy loans that do not exceed the policy's ACB will be tax free and will reduce the policy's ACB. If the policy loan exceeds the ACB, the amount borrowed in excess of the ACB will be fully taxable. There is no proportional taxation like there is with policy withdrawals.

Unlike a policy withdrawal, amounts borrowed can be repaid. If the original loan was not taxable, the repayment will merely increase the policy's ACB. If the original loan had a taxable portion, the amount repaid will be deductible from the policyholder's income, up to the previously taxed portion.

COLLATERAL ASSIGNMENT - ACCESSING YOUR TAX-FREE RETIREMENT FUNDS

While both policy withdrawals and policy loans mentioned above illicit taxation, the third way, collateral assignment, does not. It is a way of receiving your needed retirement income tax free. It is also the easiest and simplest way which is to use your policy as collateral to borrow money from a 'third party' financial institution (chartered bank).

The trick to borrowing money at favourable interest rates without having to demonstrate income, or prove your credit worthiness, is to have rock-solid collateral that is just as good, or better than, "money in the bank." And most banks consider whole life policies to be just that. So, you can "leverage" your life insurance policy to borrow *tax-free* money. And that money is not repaid until the insured dies.

This allows you to indirectly access the cash value of your policy. The primary advantage of this approach is that the proceeds can be received *tax-free.* In addition, the loan may be tax deductible if the proceeds are used to generate income from business or property. When your policy is assigned to the financial institution as a condition of the loan, a portion of the insurance costs may also be tax deductible.

WHAT TO DO WITH ALL THAT CASH

Okay, so you have tax-free cash in your hands from leveraging your $1,000,000 of cash value, so what to you do with it? You could make another tax-smart decision and buy a *prescribed annuity*. A prescribed annuity is similar to a defined benefit pension plan (those rare and disappearing pension plans that are now seen as the holy grail of pension plans) in that it guarantees you a regular income for the rest of your life (or both you and your spouse's life, if you choose that option). The big difference is it is not taxed like a pension plan, which is *taxed at 100%!* Prescribed annuities really shine when it comes to minimizing tax – and guaranteeing lifetime income.

Given that most of the income in prescribed annuities is classified as a return of capital, it would provide you with a continuous flow of income at minimal tax rates. The taxable income portion is *prescribed*—between 10% to 20% of it is taxable—and continues for the rest of your life. Depending on your tax bracket at the time, this means you could pay as low as *5% to 10% tax* on the income.

When you pass away, any outstanding loan owed to the bank that was collaterally assigned is repaid using the tax-free death benefit—remember it is life insurance. The remaining funds bypass your estate and go directly to your beneficiaries, tax-free, leaving a living legacy for your family.

This is truly a **win-win-win plan!** During your working years you grow your money *tax free*, while you use it for financing and reducing debt.

When you retire, you use your policy for a collateral assignment to receive the funds *tax-free*, so that you can buy a prescribed annuity that can earn *nearly tax-free* income for you and your spouse for as long as either of you keep breathing. And, when you are gone, the rest of your money goes to your heirs, *tax free!* The Canada Revenue Agency never sees one lucky loonie of it. That, in my books is **WINNING!**

Cash-value life insurance remains one of the best ways to achieve long-term growth, whether you leverage it or not. In most cases you won't have to make a decision on this aspect of your plan until you retire and need passive income. In the meantime, the benefits of tax-deferred growth within your policy, along with the ability to create a pool of capital to fund the things that will fund your retirement, are invaluable, as is the tax-free death-benefit payment that will pay off any outstanding loan to the bank when you die. Notice that I said *when* you die, not *if* you die. We all get our turn. All the remaining death benefit proceeds are paid directly to your individually named beneficiaries, tax-free! Since the proceeds bypass your estate, they will not be subject to pesky probate fees and the year-plus long delays and inevitable family squabbles that go along with it.

TAX-FREE WEALTH TRANSFER AT DEATH

In addition to providing you with collateral for your policy loans, the death benefit provides for your family when you are gone. Sometimes, I hear people say they do not want to leave their family rich. All they want to do is to take care of their own debts and funeral costs. Sometimes they do not even care as much as that. I have witnessed, as I am sure you have, where, because of such carelessness, they leave their family with a real mess when they are gone. The truth is no one wants their gift to their family to be anything but fond memories. For sure it is a sad day when one of the breadwinners of the family dies, but it is even sadder when their family is left in dire straits because of lack of money coming in.

Many people who have large business enterprises think that since their holdings and assets are so enormous their heirs will receive a grand reward. Instead, it can be a tangled mess of legalities that can take years of legal fees to lawyers, as well as executor fees, a decline in property value due to fire sale selloffs, and a whole pile of taxes that could reduce the estate to half, or worse, of what it took a lifetime to build. All the wealth is reduced to a fraction of what it was while the owner was alive. Their family has been cheated out of their inheritance for money owed to the CRA and for estate settlement legalities. Having life insurance keeps your wealth intact. A big fat cheque of tax-free dollars arrives in mere days for this purpose taking the pressure off your family.

It is inconsiderate and selfish to think you will not put your family in a stressful predicament if you have an untimely death. It is not about making your family rich but allowing your family time to mourn and the ability to carry on. It may be months before your loved ones are emotionally ready to resume their normal activities. Having two weeks off work before they are back at it 100 per cent does not sound realistic. If you have not provided them the financial means to care for themselves emotionally, they will be forced back to work without going through the mourning process as they should.

It is also about having a place for your family to grieve. When my dad passed away, my mom would make trips to the cemetery on the long summer days and sit under a tree beside my dad's gravesite. She did this without announcement or fanfare, whenever she felt it was important for her to have grieving time—and of course to think of all the great memories, and not so good memories, they shared together. That was her way of dealing with it. Whether it is a gravesite, or an urn memorial site, it is important your loved ones have their time and a place to have these moments.

No one buys a drill because they want a drill. They buy it because they want a hole. And no one buys life insurance because they want life insurance. They buy it because they want money when they need it most. We should all care enough about our loved ones to make sure they are taken care of after we are gone. Ben Feldman, the greatest life insurance salesperson of all time, said the miracle of life insurance is that a young person can create an estate worth millions "with the stroke of a pen and a blot of ink." I still find that statement amazing!

CHAPTER
EIGHT

BECOMING YOUR OWN BANKER

Becoming your own banker is simple and it is easy to start. Participating dividend-paying whole life insurance is the platform for IBC. When you want to take a policy loan, all you have to do is fill out a simple loan request form online. You are not at the mercy of a bank and there are no nosey credit applications. You can have the money sent to you in cheque form or directly deposited into your chequing account. You can repay your loan on your terms, and every dollar repaid is a dollar that can be used again immediately. All the while, your cash value is uninterrupted, continuing to grow 24/7/365.

Policy loans also will not affect your credit score. Even if you decide not to pay back an outstanding loan, your credit score is not affected. On the other hand, every time you request a loan from an outside lender they do a credit check. That in itself can lower your credit score. Plus, if you do not pay back your loan with these guys, not only will it put your credit score in free-fall, they will start taking legal action against you.

IT'S ALL HOW YOU THINK

As Nash repeats several times in his book, it is all in how a person thinks. The policy will not perform like a "bank" on its own. It requires actions on the part of the policy holder.

In the first chapter, I mentioned the average Canadian pays out $0.34 of every disposable dollar as an interest expense. This is not surprising given that in the first five years of an average mortgage, the amount of interest paid can be higher than what you have paid to the principal. Take for example, a 25-year mortgage of $400,000 amortizing at 4% interest. Over the first 5 years your monthly payments of $2,104.08 will total $126,244 and you will still have a mortgage balance of $348,215.71. That means only $51,784.29 has gone to principal, while $74,460.51 has gone to interest. Thus, the *volume of interest* is 59% ($74,460.51 / $126,244 x 100). This is money you will never see again! It is now the bank's loot.

But by taking a one-time a policy loan from your IBC policy of say $20,000 and plopping it down on this same mortgage you could essentially cut over $31,593 in interest costs and cut off 24 months of payments, totalling $50,497. So, with this one deposit you have potentially saved upwards of $82,000 over the length of the mortgage! Of course, you pay interest to the insurance company when repaying the loan (or more specifically you pay it to the participating fund from where you receive your dividend allotments), but now you make *extra payments* to your policy to repay the $20,000 loan. Meantime, the $20,000 you borrowed against is still compounding inside your policy.

Nelson Nash (2000), says if you take loans from your policy you should be an "honest banker" and repay them like you would if you borrowed from a bank. If you think as much of your family as you do your banker, wouldn't you repay all your loans?

You may be wondering how much interest the insurance company will charge you on your policy loan. Afterall, you want to make sure you're coming out ahead—that the rate you're paying to borrow your money doesn't defeat the purpose. Not to worry. As I will demonstrate in Chapter 10, even if your *borrowing* rate is several percentage points **higher** than the rate you are *earning,* you will still come out ahead. One of the most common misconceptions is that if you pay interest at say 6%, and earn interest at 4%, you will lose money. You won't.

So how much do insurance companies charge? It varies among insurers, and varies from year to year, but they typically charge anywhere from 4.5% to 8%. The interest may be higher or lower in the future, it really does not matter as long as the benefit you are receiving outweighs the cost. In other words, as long as your policy is growing faster than the rate you are being charged. Using our earlier example, if you are paying $4,000 or $5,000 in interest on the $20,000 you borrowed, to save $82,000 of outside mortgage costs in the long run (which would be transferred to your system), would it be worth it?

How beneficial would it be? Remember, you would be earning compound growth inside your policy on the money you borrowed, plus you would be reversing the direction your money is flowing. You would be redirecting those payments to repaying the loan in your system and charging yourself as high an interest rate as the mortgage company is charging you. How fast would your wealth grow if every dollar you were paying to a lending institution over time were reversed and going in your direction?

TAKE CONTROL

The idea behind IBC is that individuals can take control of the financing and basic banking functions in their everyday lives by reusing their dollars over and over again. Will you still use banks? Yes, of course, as explained earlier, but less and less so for financing. As you can now see, when running your dollars through your own system prior to making a purchase, and reusing these dollars, you stand to improve your financial situation.

With IBC, will you still carry debt? Yes. The difference is that, for a while at least, you will still carry *inside* debt, but your *outside* debt can diminish much more rapidly. It bears repeating that while your outside debt is disappearing, you should be an honest banker and pay your own system back. The process is to first move your outside debt to your IBC policy and then embark in systematically paying it off.

OUTSIDE DEBT VS. INSIDE DEBT

Outside debt (to a bank or other lender) is money you will never see again. Once you buy something or make a loan payment to a bank or other lender, it's gone! You got *one* use out of it! It is now in someone else's hands, never to serve you again. When you think about it, outside debt is a double-edged sword. You are both paying interest (on the money you owe) AND giving up interest (on the money you no longer have)—not a winning combination!

Inside debt works differently. Inside debt is the money you have borrowed against your policy cash values. The loan interest you are paying to the participating account, which you are a participant in, is also the same account where your next dividend originates from. It is almost like putting money in one pocket and drawing it out of the other pocket. (Of course, in actuality it's a little more complicated. The dividend scale is the outcome of a series of calculations with a number of key factors affecting its performance, including mortality, expenses, lapses, and investment returns.) Every principal dollar you repay is yours to reuse over and over again. And all the while compound growth, the "eighth wonder of the world," is working for you, uninterrupted, to grow your money.

THE TEETER-TOTTER EFFECT

Think of the two types of debt as being on a teeter-totter (see figure 1). The weight of *outside* debt is at one end forcing the board down. This is where most people are today with 34 cents, on average, of every dollar spent going to interest payments. The other end is high in the air. This is where you want to shift the debt to. Eventually, we want the board to teeter downward on this end.

Figure 1. The Teeter Totter Effect

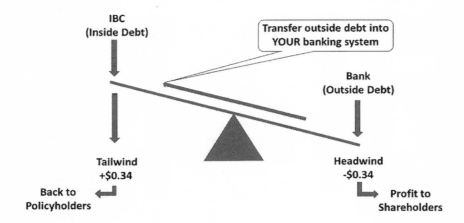

With inside debt you are getting three uses out of every dollar instead of one use like everyone else:

1. You are getting a death benefit;
2. You are having your cash value grow uninterrupted; and
3. You can use it for financing. It is turning the headwind into a tailwind!

Using your own money inside your policy and borrowing against it to pay off and eliminate debt on the outside is a worthwhile process, resulting in the teeter totter shifting over to your side. You are thinking like a banker and taking back control from the banks.

With your monthly payments increasingly going in your direction, you may need to start another policy. You can only pay back what the policy can hold up to its exempt limits, so it may take numerous policies to handle all your financing arrangements. At one time Nelson Nash had 47 policies to handle his financing and living expenses. Of course, he is the exception in that he wanted practically all his income running through a policy before he used it for other purposes.

Ideally, as shown in figure 1, you want to change the wind current from a headwind of -$0.34 pushing you backwards to a tailwind of +$0.34 pushing you forward.

The process is straight forward:

1. Deposit money into your dividend-paying participating life insurance policy.
2. Take a loan from the insurer against your policy.
3. Use that money to pay out an existing outside loan or living expense.
4. Pay off the debt in your own system.

You can use this process to pay cash for vehicles or any other purchase you make, or to even pay your monthly expenses after debt is gone, while still having your own money grow uninterrupted.

When you take out a policy loan, the insurance company uses your policy as collateral and uses the death benefit as security. Will they ever demand you pay back your loan? No. You are not obligated to pay it back. If you died before paying it back, anything outstanding will simply be subtracted from the death benefit and the remaining funds will be paid directly to your beneficiaries, tax free. To your loved ones, you still leave them *pennies from heaven.*

Of course, to keep your policy growing efficiently, and to keep your policy from lapsing for lack of funds, you should pay back your policy loan. But, since life is not perfect, and stuff happens, IBC gives you the flexibility to pay it back, or not, when you choose. You may suffer a job loss or have health issues. That is life. That is the power of being your own banking source. You control that process!

Nash (2000, 35) states clearly, "Anytime you eliminate the payment of interest to others and direct that *same market rate of interest* to an entity that you own and control, which is subject to minimal taxation (life insurance companies do pay taxes), you have improved your situation."

CHAPTER
NINE

ECONOMIC VALUE ADDED (EVA)

Before being introduced to the concept of "economic value added" (EVA), corporations were borrowing capital from banks and paying interest. They were treating their own capital as if it had no cost. (Like many people do today with their own money). They were underutilizing it. Then, in the 1970s, one bright person said, "Why not loan our own capital for a new expansion and charge interest to that division? If the new division overruns their costs, they pay us for that, too!" The idea caught on quickly in the corporate world. Their lost-opportunity costs disappeared, and profitability increased dramatically.

The importance of not interrupting compound interest cannot be overstated. Multinational companies realized that paying themselves for using their own money added value to their corporate dollars. The concept of putting value on their own money, EVA, caught on.

While companies have flourished under this model, most people have not realized its value for individuals. Many Canadians have been taught that *withdrawing* their money and *paying cash* for everything is the best way to make purchases. You hear this from financial gurus like Dave Ramsey, whose widespread financial program is broadcast daily throughout North America and is taught in churches across the continent. While his "pay cash, never go in debt" advice has helped people stay out of financial trouble, he asks you to treat your own capital the same way companies did before discovering EVA—as if it has no cost! The Nelson Nash Institute has pointed out the flaws in his approach numerous times. Following Ramsey's advice will get you *one* use out of every dollar, and then that money is gone. Will you ever see that money again? You will not.

It is obvious to everyone that you give up interest when you withdraw money from a savings account, but seldom do you hear the general public or financial advisors mention there is a cost in doing so. Yet the alternate use of money must always be considered. What are the opportunity costs?

EVA FOR OURSELVES

Similarly, to the way companies acted before using EVA, most people today act as if their money has no value. We must remind ourselves that our own capital has a cost. Think of EVA this way and the money in your pocket will take on new meaning.

If you borrow money from a bank, you pay them back what you borrowed plus interest. The same is true with a credit card; you must pay them interest. But, if you use your own money, you never think to pay yourself interest. Why not? When you stop your money from growing—by withdrawing it, instead of taking a loan against it—you are declaring that your money is not worth as much as another person's money.

The fundamental aspect of IBC is realizing that just like a corporation, your money has economic value, too! This is realized by letting your money continue to grow while you take a loan against it.

IBC: A PLACE FOR WINDFALLS

Nelson Nash realized the concept of EVA applied not just to corporations, but to his own circumstances. At one point in his life, he received a windfall from selling a piece of land he had owned on the edge of his home city, Birmingham, Alabama, for many years. The windfall was of "Grand Canyon" size! What did he do with the money? Where did he put it? Where would you put it if you had a ginormous windfall and wanted to keep it safe and in a place with near perfect tax consequences? Would you risk it if you were at retirement age when this happened? Would you stick your money into a bank? A mutual fund? Would you buy another property? Would you take a dream vacation with your family anywhere your heart desired?

Of course, the obvious answer would be that he started another policy on a family member who was insurable, since he was uninsurable at the time. (You can own a life insurance policy on another family member, where the death benefit is underwritten on that life if you, yourself, are "uninsurable".) But, that is not what he did. He already owned numerous policies on his children and grandchildren. Here is what Nash did after receiving the windfall. He *paid off policy loans!*

Imagine that!

He knew his land would sell some day and be worth much more than he had originally paid for it, so over time he dramatically increased his life insurance premiums, creating a pool of cash values from which to borrow against so he could eventually pay off the bank loans he owed (Nash, 2000, 13). Nash continued to start new policies and almost immediately took loans out on them, knowing this made perfect sense. He knew he would repay the loans over time. If he passed away in the interim, the death benefits on all the policies would wipe out the outstanding policy loans, and there would still be the remaining death benefit passed on to his wife and family, tax-free.

When he received the windfall, he was not making a premium payment, he was merely depositing it into the policies to reduce the outstanding balance on loans they had been advancing to him over the years. He was utilizing the IBC concept flawlessly. He wanted to be free and clear of outside bank loans and over the years shifted them to his policies. Of course, he had a *system of policies* to accomplish this, knowing that someday the land would sell. Nash seceded from the way most of the world was behaving by understanding how dividend-paying whole life insurance works, and by realizing this was the ideal place to warehouse his medium of exchange. Like Nash, those practising IBC usually do not have one policy, but a system of policies to accommodate financing needs as they arise.

Question: *While the loans were outstanding was he still earning interest and dividends on his cash value in his policies during all those years?*

Answer: Yes, the cash value that was used as collateral continued to grow as though no loans were outstanding.

Question: *Was he paying the insurance company interest for the loans he had accumulated?*

Answer: Yes, he was paying interest to the insurance company for the loans. The interest could either accumulate or he could make interest-only payments to the insurance company. When the windfall came he paid down the principal.

Question: *Did he come out ahead in the end?*

Answer: As Nash says, "Anytime that you can cut out the payment of interest to others and direct that same market rate of interest to an entity that you own and control…with minimal taxation… then you have improved your situation."

Knowing how dividend-paying life insurance works is an essential ingredient, since "…the central message is not about real estate—it is about the magic of leverage" (Nash, 2000, 12). Nash (2000, 37) has often said that calling it "life insurance" is a poor name. He would prefer to call it a "banking system with a death benefit thrown in for good measure".

CHAPTER

TEN

UNDERSTANDING LOANS: COMPOUND INTEREST VS AMORTIZING INTEREST

To illustrate the importance of having uninterrupted compounded growth on your cash value, even though you are still paying borrowing costs, picture this:

- You have $30,000 in a savings account earning **4%** annually and you want to withdraw the money to buy a car.
- The advisor tells you it is better to take a loan for $30,000, repay the loan at **6%** interest and leave the 4% savings account alone.
- You can repay the loan with monthly instalments over the next five years.

What should you do? Should you take the loan and pay 6% interest or withdraw the cash which is earning 4%?

Most people would withdraw the cash, basing their decision on the fact the loan is *two percentage points higher than the savings rate*. That is what many gurus tell us to do, saying, "It is better to pay cash!"

Well, let's do the math.

As shown in table 1, after five years your **4% savings** grew to $36,500. **You earned $6,500 in interest.**

Table 1. Saving $30,000, compounding annually at 4% over 5 years

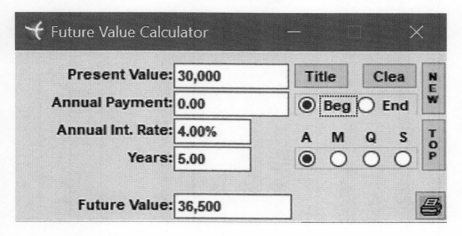

In table 2, you can see your total **6% loan repayment** was $34,626 ($577.10 x 60 mos.). Therefore, **your loan cost you only $4,626 in interest.**

What is the result? You gained $1,874 by taking the loan and letting your 4% savings compound ($6,500 interest earned - $4,625 interest paid = $1,874 gain)!

Table 2. Borrowing $30,000, paying 6% over 5 years

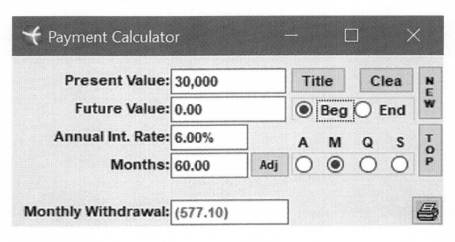

Note: The only way this example could produce better results is if you could replace the old savings account with a new one that was guaranteed to pay 4% on _monthly_ deposits for five years. Then, in five years, you would be slightly ahead by withdrawing the original savings and replenishing it with the same monthly payment you would make for the loan repayment. But, where do you find an account paying 4% on monthly payments? Outside of getting 3% to 5% on cash values inside a properly structured IBC policy (a reasonable long-term rate on the cash value using the current dividend scales) I have not found one.

As stated before, one of the most common misconceptions is that if you pay interest at say 6%, and earn interest at 4%, that the 6% paid would be a larger number. **It is not.** _The 4% earned will result in significantly more dollars than the 6% interest paid over the same time period._ The reason for this is that you _pay amortizing interest_ on a declining balance each month and _earn compounding interest_ on an increasing balance. Let that sink in.

Upon seeing this example, we must re-think the idea of paying cash. Money has a cost. Withdrawing cash, especially from a compounding interest type of account found inside a properly deigned IBC policy, must be scrutinized before doing so. This is one of the most common mistakes that is made in the financial world, something that even renowned financial gurus repeatedly overlook!

LOST-OPPORTUNITY COST

Letting your cash continue to compound uninterrupted in a tax-free environment is a huge advantage – even more so over longer time periods of 10, 20, and 30 years! Not doing so, is called lost-opportunity cost.

Do financial institutions give you this advice for:

+ your car loans?
+ your retirement or investment planning?
+ your emergency needs?
+ your equipment purchases?

They do not! Yet, you can put more money in your pocket when you take a loan against an asset that continues earning interest, than if you cashed in the asset and started over.

The Infinite Banking Concept is not a loophole or an oversight. Its unique components set it apart from any other wealth creation vehicle you can find. You have better control, more guarantees, more access to your money, and less risk than with conventional investments. That is why wealthy people, politicians, business owners, trades people, professionals and day care workers are joining the growing number of Canadians using IBC! It puts you in the driver's seat. These people have experienced a permanent mental shift in the way they think about their own personal economy: opting for cash flow over net worth; utilization over accumulation; and abundance, where scarcity existed before.

Think of playing a sport. It is only fun if you know the rules. If you don't know the rules it is not fun, and you can't play the game well. When you know the rules, everything starts to make sense. Now you can play the game and win!

WHY HAVE I NOT HEARD OF THIS BEFORE?

People ask us, *"Why haven't I heard of this before?"* First, Nelson Nash did not write his book *Becoming Your Own Banker,* until 2000. Second, while the number of IBC practitioners has been growing since that time, and the word has been rapidly spreading, we have not yet reached the tipping point to affect the masses. Third, most people don't think of life insurance as an *asset.* When people think of life insurance they think *term insurance* because that's what they've been taught. Term insurance is an *expense.* You will never see those dollars again. There is no cash value and only 1% of term insurance is ever paid out in claims. You get one use out of your dollar and it is gone. Not so for whole-life policies which, when designed properly, will pay out the death benefit 100% of the time as long as you keep it in force. Next to your house, it becomes one of the best assets you can own. In my opinion, many advisors who ascribe only to term life insurance either do not yet know about how IBC works, or are associated with companies that do not offer a suitable whole life product. Though many insurers offer whole life products, only a few are flexible enough for this purpose.

To become an authorized IBC practitioner an advisor is required to take an eight-unit study course designed by the Nelson Nash Institute out of Alabama in the US. It has been the most sensible and real-world course ever in my many years as a financial advisor. It can take one to three months to complete the course, depending on the time you put into it. US life insurance companies are similar to Canadian companies in many respects and the concept works seamlessly on both sides of the border. There are some differences in taxation and policy design, but these can be readily compensated for. Not many Canadian advisors have yet taken the course although the numbers are increasing. As a result, clients are still hearing financial "experts" tell them they should lock their money into investments that restrict their money's uses or penalizes them for accessing their money!

The other question I hear almost daily is, "Why didn't you teach me this 20 years ago?" Well, I think to myself, "Twenty years ago I didn't know this stuff; and 20 years ago, I didn't know you." Who knows, maybe you were not looking for this stuff either? You know the old saying: "When the student is ready, the teacher will appear." It is funny to me how we can stumble upon things in our lives that can completely shift our thinking, making our lives that much better from that point forward. IBC is an economic paradigm: changing thinking, changing lives.

CHAPTER
ELEVEN

MY STORY

*"If your outgo exceeds your income,
then your upkeep will be your downfall."*

— Unknown

No one likes a pastor who claims to be sinless. I openly admit I have been just as susceptible to financial disasters as other people. I have been careless in the past and can talk from experience about the financial headwinds having their way with me and my family. Nothing I seemed to do would help. The banks owned me and had me in such tight bondage, I could not afford to take a breather, let alone a holiday.

I, and my wonderful wife, Sue, who I adore and who is a real trooper, having stood by me through the good, the bad and the ugly, have had to stand up against a mountain of debt which could have swallowed us whole at any second. We had three kids to raise and three mortgages to pay, on three different properties, in a declining real estate market. The pressure was enormous.

On top of that, we owned a business (outside of my financial business) that, after being manipulated by outside forces, ended in failure, costing us a fortune. Sue had left her well-paying job 17 years before to be a stay-at-home mom. And, because we had more holes in our cash flow bucket than we could handle, the money was leaking out faster than we could keep pouring it in.

Sleepless nights would make it hard for us to stay productive the following days: two or three sleepless nights in a row and soon the whole week, or month, was unproductive. It left us wondering if we would ever get back to the peaceful, happy life we had started out with in our marriage.

It was overwhelming. It felt like every time we took a step forward, we would go *backwards* two steps. We were facing a *headwind* (as I would later learn from Nelson Nash). Close to 80% of our debt payments were going to pay interest.

We had lost control and found ourselves in rough waters, but we started to chart out our course, the only way we knew how: by working harder to make a lot more money. Thankfully, we did start earning more. The headwind of interest payments became less severe and with persistence, we paid off bigger chunks of debt. Our financial wind currents started to change, making our course a little easier to navigate. The headwind, once a gale, now became more like an annoying draft, reminding us it was still there; though our situation was improving, we were still being held by debt.

Every now and then our bank would send us a statement—a "Who's Your Daddy?" statement—reminding us they were still in charge. Like Alice in Wonderland, we were running as fast as we could to stay in the same place. It took us over a decade, but gradually we gained more command of our ship.

It was only later, after learning about the Infinite Banking Concept, that I began to realize we could have done things much easier, much quicker, and more efficiently than we had. Still, once I did discover IBC, it was much smoother sailing. We finally found ourselves with a tailwind. It's too bad we had charted so much of our course the hard way.

My hope for you, in reading this book now, is that you will not have to struggle like my wife and I did. You will know how to use that tailwind to help you chart the best possible course in the easiest, quickest and most efficient way—the IBC way.

A HORROR STORY

Recently, I met a young couple with a mortgage, three young children and two dogs. They both work outside the home and they are both good people, but they are struggling to make ends meet. In need of reliable wheels, they went to a corner car dealership. When the deal was finalized, they walked away with a three-year-old Ford Fusion and a debt of $24,000. With their credit now maxed out, they have no room for mistakes or unexpected expenses. And that is not the nightmare. It's the interest they are paying to the finance company for their loan that is keeping them up at night!

With an interest rate of 29% and payments of $630 per month, it will take them eight years to pay off the car! Think about it. Payments of $630 per month, totaling $60,480, for a $24,000 Ford Fusion! The interest they will pay is $36,476! This means the *volume of interest* is 60% ($36,476 / $60,480 = 0.60). So, they're really paying 60% not 29%, which is the *rate* of interest. And, they will be paying more than two-and-a-half times what the car is worth because of *interest alone!*

Amazing! I wonder if the salesperson and the owner of the corner car lot, who both knew the couple's situation, felt like they were doing a service for these customers, or if they felt like they had just pulled off an *armed robbery?* It is insane! Please do not get me wrong. I am not blaming most car-sales people. Every industry has a few bad-asses. Thankfully, the majority are upstanding and good people providing a needed service to their customers.

What I find most amazing is that it is legal to charge 29% in this low-interest-rate environment. But we can't be so naïve as to think that lenders are not out for blood. They would eat their young if they could. Of course, the couple were charged this rate as a result of having had bad credit, but more importantly they agreed to it, not understanding basic economics. Are you not proud of our education system where you can graduate from high school knowing how to dissect a frog and calculate the square root of 100, but not knowing basic financing? Where was the class in that?

Realizing their situation, this couple did try to consolidate the loan at their regular bank. Unfortunately, they got turned down, so for now they are greasing the wheels of the auto-financing industry. But, if mortgage rates increase by a percentage or two (and they likely will!) when this couple goes to renew their mortgage, they could face losing their house. If you think this is an extreme example, I can tell you I have seen my fair share of similar financing horror stories.

Let me ask you a question. Is there more profit margin on the *sale* of a car or on its *financing*? If you said financing, you get to be salesperson of the month! Financing, as an industry, is extremely profitable, and this is one reason why thinking like a banker is a must!

If this couple had known about IBC four to five years earlier and had been putting that same $630 per month into a policy during that time, how different would life be for them now? They could have been in a position to use their own money as collateral for that car loan. The approximately $2,600 in interest to the insurance company could have been more than compensated for inside the policy, which would keep growing while they paid the $630 per month back to their policy for the next 3.5 years. (On the other hand, they could decide not to repay the policy loan, or just pay the interest only.)

After 3.5 years, they could have paid off the loan and every nickel they borrowed would be available to them to borrow again. They could have knocked off 4 years of payments, ended up with the car, *and* all the money they paid for the car! Imagine the difference this would make over their lifetime if they bought all their future vehicles this way!

> A person's mind, **stretched by a new idea**, never goes back to its original dimensions.
>
> —Oliver Wendell Holmes Jr.

WHAT IS YOUR STORY?

Even people who are not indebted to high-interest-rate financers are at risk. With bank interest rates on the low end, people are putting themselves into more and more debt. Today, $1.68 is what the average Canadian spends over and above a dollar earned.. That money goes to pay their mortgage, food, gas, cell, utilities, insurance, car payments, credit card debt, lines of credit, etc. So, when interest rates rise, which we are witnessing today, what is going to happen?

In the past year and a half, as of this writing, there were three interest-rate hikes, and you can bet it will not stop there. As interest rates climb higher and higher, how many people will falter under the pressure? How many people will lose their homes along with their sense of self-worth?

Even with interest rates as low as they are, I find myself running into people shackled by the extent of their debt. It is easy to see why. Again, let's say you have a 25-year, $300,000 mortgage at 3.5% interest. You would be paying $1,493.05 per month, and after five years, you would have made payments totaling $89,583. Unfortunately, only $41,302 of that total has gone to reduce the loan. This means that $48,281 has gone to interest. In other words, 54% of every dollar you paid out went to the cost of financing!

If you sell the house in that first five years, it gets even worse. Then the proportion of your money going to interest never gets better because you take on a new mortgage and the process is repeated. As Nash says, "He thinks he is buying a house, but all he is doing is making the wheels of the banking business and real estate business turn."

So, what happens in this same scenario when interest rates increase?

On the same 25-year, $300,000 mortgage, if the interest rate jumped to 5.5%, you would now be paying $1,818.34 per month. That would total $109,100 in payments, with only $32,732 going to reduce the loan. This means $76,368 has gone to interest. In other words, now 70% of every dollar paid out would go to the cost of financing!

From what I have read online, the Canadians' debt ratio is climbing every year and this ratio will only multiply when interest rates increase as they are expected to! More and more of our dollars will be required to pay debt, along with the interest it steals from us. This is very troublesome, but the effects can be thwarted by acting now. By creating your own pool of wealth inside a policy and taking policy loans when your mortgage renews at a higher rate, the money you have accumulated can then be used to pay down lump sums on your mortgage, redirecting those payments back to you. By using policy loans to pay lump sums toward your mortgage each year, you can change the wind current in your direction.

CHAPTER

TWELVE

WHERE NOT TO SEEK INVESTING ADVICE

If you ask people what they think about the advice coming from television's financial pundits, you will get a mixed feedback. Much of what emerges from these 24-hour news cycles can either put you to sleep or leave your head spinning. Unless you are attuned to listening to the financial markets daily, the sound penetrating your ears may be akin to how elevator music sounds to a heavy metalist. And, the information given has no inherent value whatsoever.

While the commentators are well-dressed, articulate and well-meaning, the advice they are giving can range from fair to useless. Opinions about stock picking, trading maneuvers and market predictions are freely given, but solid, balanced information is usually in short supply.

Sometimes the things they say have a hint of truth, and sound reasonable and believable. Then, someone else responds and waters it down with economic data that was just released about jobs or consumer credit or some other factoring influence. Everyday there is something new, and while many investors love this stuff, heaven only knows what they get out of it. Much of it is noise and keeping up with television ratings.

We have seen dot-com bubbles, overinflated housing markets and runaway bull markets. We have also seen every market gain over a ten-year period disappear almost overnight from over-optimism and speculation, followed by panic.

As Vira Vermond says, "The same kind of thing keeps happening over and over. We make the same mistakes. ... Booms and busts just happen to involve different timelines and people" ("Where not to seek investing advice," *Globe and Mail*, April 23, 2018).

Historically, we know this is true. If a bust happens in a timeline that does not align with your retirement goals, in other words, if the market crashes just before your retirement, or once you have started drawing on your portfolio, do you have any recourse? Can you wait it out and delay your retirement until the market rebounds? Or, if you are already retired when it does happen, can you go back to work? What actionable steps can you take when you know something is coming? Most people do not have answers for this, and their options are limited.

In the end, you cannot predict the market. Vermond's article ends with a quote from Dan Solin: *"Markets are basically random.... So how are we supposed to predict where the markets are headed?"*

The advice here is that instead of focusing on what is being said on the television business channels by the gurus, focus on what you actually have control over. What savings vehicles are right for you and your long-term goals, and that minimize and defer taxes to the greatest extent, and where you can diversify your holdings to alleviate risk?

If you do not have control over how your money is expected to grow over the next 10, 20, 30, and 40 years, or if your current portfolio could drop significantly when the market crashes, it is time to take a stern look at how a properly designed IBC plan can compete with what you are presently banking on for your future.

RISK DOES NOT EQUAL REWARD

The financial industry has convinced Canadians (and it has been given wings by the media) that you must take higher risks to receive greater rewards. We have been taught that the stock market is the place to put money. As an employee, you may have a company defined contribution pension plan, or a group RRSP, where the only option is the stock market. If you own your own business, investment advisors will also lead you in the direction of the stock market, or private equity world. It has been good for the companies listed on the stock market and for the people trying to raise private equity, but has it been good for you?

Risk does not equal reward. Advisors are taught that risk is necessary and are encouraged to show their clients various options, few of which offer guarantees. Many times, clients end up experiencing huge losses, paying too many fees, and worst of all, running out of time to start all over again. The emotional toll it takes can cause health and family relationship challenges that can last a lifetime, or even shorten your lifetime.

I have seen it firsthand and have been guilty of receiving, and thus giving poor advice. Far higher risks exist in the private equity world of exempt markets, than in stock markets, where countless numbers of investors have seen their money all but disappear. Knowing that you have given a client an option, and upon taking that option they have lost money with little likelihood of recovering it anytime soon (if at all), is devastating for both the client and the advisor. It may take the client decades to recover from such a setback and those years cannot be recovered. Meanwhile, your relationship as "trusted advisor" to your client quickly dissolves.

It was not long before I found I do not have the stomach for it and soon after gave up my license in that field. Even though clients, knowing full well the risks involved, and while they may have been willing to sign "risk acknowledgement agreements," many of these clients were not cut out for it either. Investors can only make decisions based on the limited information we advisors are knowledgeable about, and the printed material that goes along with it.

One of the great oxymoronic names of our times is the official name of the certificate required for advisors to provide such risk-laden advice. It is called a "securities license." I find I can sleep much better knowing that I no longer have to put my clients' money at such risk in attempts to grow their wealth. After learning the hard way, I have little tolerance for losing money: mine or my clients'! My own personal risk tolerance is next to ZERO.

Regularly we receive emails or calls from good folks, wanting to take high risks because some seemingly informed person gave them a hot tip. They ask if we would recommend it or something similar. We answer with a quote from Andrew Redleaf (2010, 47), author of *Panic: The Betrayal Of Capitalism*:

> The notion that risk equals reward is worse than a myth—it's a mass delusion, a mass delusion that in our time has cost investors trillions of dollars… It has lulled an entire generation of financial advisors into complacency about the risk to which they expose their clients… In the real economy, risk is manifestly not the source of wealth but the great destroyer.

We could not agree more!

The risk-based methods of planning your financial "security" are everywhere and are snowballing at alarming rates. Risk does not equal reward. In my personal experience risk equals loss.

Most of us are conditioned, early in life by "advisors," friends or the media, how to invest. We end up *paying too many fees*, experiencing *huge losses*, and worst of all, *running out of time* to start all over again. The emotional toll it takes can cause health and family challenges that can last a lifetime.

I have seen it firsthand. I have been guilty of it. I have witnessed and felt the trauma, the anxiety and the brokenness some of these "too good to be true" high risk investments end up like—nightmarish, entangled legal messes. I will never go down that road again, and you do not have to!

IBC's platform is one of the safest in history. Backed by one of the most stable financial entities in the country—life insurance companies—IBC has the highest number of guarantees *any* advisor can offer, making it one of the least risky places to keep and grow your wealth. With IBC, and using participating dividend-paying life insurance, you do not have to take on risk to receive competitive growth and great benefits.

DID YOUR BROKER MISLEAD YOU?

The stock market at the end of February 2018, and again in October 2018, saw volatility like they haven't seen in years. Many financial pundits speculate a major crash is soon to follow and warn investors to move to safety. This seesawing of the market is its nature. So, let's take a look at the "unintended" consequences of volatility and how it affects your money.

Over the last 30 years the standard deviation (which measures the ups and downs) of the TSX has been 16%, according to a publication by Canada Life (*Historical Performance*, 46-6401-6/17). *Volatility* of the stock market is what kills the growth in your portfolio if your RRSP, or tax-free savings account (TFSA) is invested there. Often, new clients show us their existing portfolios, which they have accumulated with a previous advisor, and ask, "Why is there not more money in my RRSP account when my average return is showing 7.5% per year?" The answer is volatility.

Volatility erodes market returns. Brokers and advisors prefer to quote *average* rates of returns, perhaps because the average rates of return look and sound better than the compounded annual growth rate (CAGR), which is the *actual* rate of return. The difference is best explained by Hans Wagner and I thank my friend Kim Butler for introducing his work to me. In the article, *"Did Your Broker Mislead You"* (March 1, 2018) Wagner writes, "Imagine you have $10,000. This year, your $10,000 grows 100%, leaving you with $20,000. The following year, your investment falls 50%, taking you back to your original amount, $10,000. Over the years, your annualized gain is ZERO." So, the 0% you received would be the CAGR or actual rate of return.

In this scenario, the advisor, eager to put some positive spin on the situation, may tell you that your average return is 25% (100% - 50% / 2 years = 25%). That number is correct. And very misleading! If you made 25% would your portfolio not be 25% bigger than when you started? In real life, you can only realize the CAGR, not the average annual returns many brokers and advisors claim. As Wagner correctly states, the culprit is market volatility.

In truth, the more volatility experienced by the market, the larger the *drop* in the compound (or actual) return. In other words, the more volatile the market, the lower the actual investment return will be. This is because whenever you lose money, it takes a greater return to just break even. Wagner states, "If you lose 20% you must earn 25% to get back to where you began." So, the more you lose, the worse the situation gets. Lose 50% and you must double your money (grow it by 100%) to get back to even.

Question: *In the stock market, is it easier to lose 50% or to gain 100%?* I think you know the answer. And just as importantly, it does not matter if the losses or gains come first. Reversing the order gives the same result.

HOW CAN YOU GUARD AGAINST VOLATILITY?

This is where the true value of using IBC comes in. It is obvious that we should allocate our assets to those that are not correlated to the stock market, since CAGR works only when there are NO negative returns. In other words, CAGR can only work when the yearly results are either positive or ZERO, but never negative. One of the major reasons why dividend paying whole-life policies are an ideal platform for IBC is because the cash value can never have a negative year. The worst-case scenario would be a ZERO-dividend year! That said, your existing cash value would not go down. In fact, it would continue to rise incrementally because you are still guaranteed daily interest, regardless of the dividend.

AVERAGE IS NOT THE SAME AS CAGR

Suppose you asked your brother-in-law, "Should I invest in a portfolio with a 6.74%, 19 year *average* return, or in one with a 4% *compounded annual growth rate?*" He would probably say, "Take the 6.74%! It's silly to take the 4% and lose 2.74%!" Yet, he would be giving you bad advice. The question that needs to be asked is: "Did the 'average return' experience any negative returns during any of those 19 years?" If it experienced a negative year, the 6.74% *average return* becomes meaningless!

To further demonstrate the difference between CAGR and average rate of return, I compiled the last 19 years worth of listed returns on the S&P/TSX composite total return index. You can see the results in table 3 below.

Table 3: Compound annual growth rate (CAGR) vs. average returns (S&P/TSX composite index returns include the reinvestment of dividends).

Year	S&P TSX Composite Index	Fund Values	CAGR 4%	Fund Values
2000	7.41%	105,262	4%	104,000
2001	(12.57%)	90,190	4%	108,160
2002	(12.44%)	77,391	4%	112,486
2003	26.72%	96,108	4%	116,986
2004	14.48%	107,824	4%	121,665
2005	24.13%	131,165	4%	126,532
2006	17.26%	150,728	4%	131,593
2007	9.83%	162,234	4%	136,857
2008	(33.00%)	106,523	4%	142,331
2009	35.05%	140,982	4%	148,024
2010	17.61%	162,493	4%	153,945
2011	(8.71%)	145,373	4%	160,103
2012	7.19%	152,709	4%	166,507
2013	12.99%	169,095	4%	173,168
2014	10.60%	183,278	4%	180,094
2015	(8.72%)	163,950	4%	187,298
2016	20.75%	194,011	4%	194,790
2017	8.92%	207,090	4%	202,582
2018	(9.40%)	183,952	4%	210,685
TOTAL	6.74%	$183,952	4%	$210,685
Avg.	6.74%	(2% Fees)	4%	(No Fees)
CAGR	3.26%		4%	

As you can see in table 3, if you invested $100,000 in the S&P/TSX (**risky & volatile**) in 2000, by the end of 2018, with an average return of 6.74%, and annual fees of 2%, you would have accumulated **$183,952.**

Remarkably, in the **safer dollar portfolio** "compounding annually" at 4% (a reasonable long-term rate of return on deposits into a properly structured IBC plan, *after the cost of insurance*), you would have accumulated an impressive **$210,685! You beat the TSX/S&P index by over 26,733, after fees, with a 4% CAGR!**

The point here is that the *average rate of return* of 6.74% is very misleading. It is NOT the same as CAGR! So, what is the real rate of return after fees with the TSX/S&P? The real rate of return (or CAGR) to accumulate $183,952, after fees, is a mere 3.26%. Isn't it interesting how the stock market seems to get all the attention and is highly rated as the go-to place where your wealth should reside, while a dividend paying life insurance policy, which when structured properly can produce competitive returns, gets little attention. Properly structured dividend paying whole life insurance is one of the best kept secrets in Canada.

It goes without saying that if you can achieve CAGR that is safe, liquid and accessible, without interrupting its growth, even while you use it, then that is a good place to park your cash in any environment. Besides having numerous other guarantees, this is one of the reasons why practitioners of IBC recommend dividend paying whole life insurance where—*even after the cost of insurance*—3% to 5% CAGR is a reasonable long-term rate of return on your money.

Still, some of you may be thinking that 3% to 5% CAGR is not very exciting. I agree that it would be more exciting to have your money double and triple in 90 days, or 2 years, or 5 years, but that is not called investing, it is called gambling. I am not saying you should not gamble. But it only makes sense to gamble when you have excess funds, so that the gamble only represents a small portion of your total net worth.

LET'S NOT FORGET MANAGEMENT FEES

We touched on management fees in the above example. Now, let's look at what the true cost really is for those fees. Management expense ratios (MERs) can really do a number on your mutual funds, or managed portfolio results.

Even when being conservative showing MERs at 2%, the results are astounding. Many mutual fund fees charge higher than 2% to cover:

1. sales charges (paid by you)
2. management fees and operating expenses (MER – paid by the fund)
3. trailing commissions to the advisor (included in the MER)

First, let's compare investing $20,000 per year for 35 years using the last 35 years of the TSX/S&P Total Return. We will assume a tax rate of 24% with a dividend credit for losses. Using Truth Concepts trusted calculators, the results look like this:

- With 0% MER, if you invested straight into the S&P/TSX, your total accumulation would come to $2,092,614.
- However, with 2% MER, if you invested straight into the S&P/TSX, your total accumulation would come to $1,411,068.

So, the *true cost* of the MER – because these monies could not be invested since day one – is $681,546 ($2,092,614 - $1,411,068 = $681,546).

When we put this into perspective having a MER of 2% (which is conservative), the reduction in your portfolio over 35 years and paying for MERs is 48.3% ($681,546 / $1,411,068 x 100 = 48.3%).

Looking at a 48.3% reduction in your retirement fund after 35 years shows you the real impact of what a 2% MER can have. Since most people own mutual funds wouldn't it be a good idea to know what the impact of the fees they are paying will have?

Our clients enjoy looking at illustrations showing the cash value of specially designed dividend paying life insurance year by year, and how it stacks up against a mutual fund portfolio year by year after the cost of insurance. Usually, it doesn't take long, only a few years, before the insurance policy starts to gain momentum on the mutual fund since there are no fees or taxes to contend with – not to mention all the other benefits and guarantees that come with life insurance.

Mutual fund fees take a substantial bite out of your portfolio. The average total cost of ownership of mutual funds for clients using advice-based distribution channels in Canada at the end of 2016 was 1.96% when taxes were excluded. Then, there are usually advisor fees on top of that.

MERs are charged regardless of whether the market goes up or down. This means that if the market drops and you lose money, the fund managers still get paid. If the markets drop and you lose money, the advisors still gets paid. But what about you? You are the only one putting up the money. You hold all the risk of investing it, and yet you are the only one not getting paid and you lose the money you had when the market drops. Anything broken with this picture?

THE PERFECT TAX PLAN

Will taxes go up, or will they go down? If you say, "They will likely go up," I am with you. The marginal tax rate in Canada is likely to increase. So, does it make sense to save for retirement by cramming money into your RRSPs every year when taxes are likely to increase by the time you need to take out your investments? If taxes do in fact go up over time, how much sense would it make to take money out of your paycheque today at a 25% to 30% tax rate, only to defer your tax and take it out when you retire, paying a tax rate of 35% to 40% or higher? Would it make sense? Let me answer for you. No!

So, what I am saying is, if you are an employee, it makes sense to continue putting money into your Registered Pension Plan (RPP) or RRSP up to the limit the company is matching for you. But, for anything beyond that you need to think about *tax diversification*. Everybody thinks about asset allocation and asset diversification but what about tax diversification? If you think about it, most baby boomers have almost all their money sitting in registered plans that are *completely* taxable when they retire. So, anywhere from a quarter to nearly half of your income goes to 'big brother' CRA!

A better strategy for tax diversification, as well as asset diversification and asset allocation, would be to put the larger portion of your savings into a permanent dividend-paying life insurance policy. Why? Because when done correctly, you can receive nearly all of the cash value when you retire, or for that matter whenever you want, without suffering the cost of paying tax. (TFSAs are also an option, but other than tax-free growth and tax-free withdrawal they do not offer the extent of the benefits offered by the life insurance policy. And here again, with most TFSAs we are talking about risk, and you are also limited in the amount you can contribute to them). The best years in your life insurance policy as far as cash value growth, and death benefit growth, just happen to be those years when you need passive income for retirement. And, all those years leading up to your retirement, the cash value was easily accessible for financing.

What would a perfect *tax* plan look like?

1. Get a *tax deduction* on every dollar you deposit to your plan.
2. Then, have it grow *tax deferred* year after year, for decades!
3. Finally, when you retire you get it out *tax-free*.

That would be the *perfect tax plan*. Unfortunately, the perfect tax plan does not exist. You can either have one or two, or two or three, but you cannot have *one, two and three*.

With an RRSP or RPP you get *one* and *two*: a tax deduction when you contribute and a tax hit when you withdraw it. Every dollar out is subject to tax. With life insurance or a TFSA you get *two* and *three*: get no deduction when you contribute and pay no tax when you withdraw it. That is how an IBC plan works. You do not get a tax deduction on the money you contribute to it, but you *can access the money tax-free at retirement, using a collateral assignment, when the time rolls around*. If you diversify your taxes, rather than having it all in a taxable account, you will have a lot more spending money in retirement and will have come close to a perfect tax plan.

CHAPTER

THIRTEEN

IN SEARCH OF THE PERFECT INVESTMENT

Knowing the perfect *tax* plan does not exist, but that you can get close to it, let's look at what a *perfect investment* would look like. If you were to design your perfect plan of where to keep your money, what attributes would you give it? The answers below originate from Lara, Murphy, and Nash (2018, 16-18) in *The Case for IBC*, from surveys they took with attendees at their seminars.

High Returns: The first thing most people say is that they want the market value of their investment to increase significantly over time.

Consistent Rate of Return: When pressed, most people will further explain that not only is it desirable to have a high rate of return on *average*, but if we are talking the "perfect investment" they want that high rate of return to be *consistent*. They are saying if investment A and investment B both yielded an XX percent return per year over the course of 10 years, they would prefer to hold the investment that was more predictable, year to year.

Conservative (Safe): This is a logical extension of the desire for consistency. People want an investment that goes *up*. Once it reaches a particular market value, they do not want it to be able to go down from there. Remember, the "eighth wonder of the world", compound interest, only works when there are no negative years!

Liquid: It is one thing to know your investment is "worth" a certain amount of money, but it is another thing to be able to *convert it into dollars* should the need arise. A liquid asset can be sold for its market value to raise cash very quickly.

Guaranteed: Some assets come with actual guarantees put out by reputable and strong institutions, so naturally the "perfect investment" would too.

Tax Benefits (Tax Free): Ideally, our hypothetical investment would not significantly increase our tax liability. In a perfect world, we would enjoy all of its other benefits without suffering any tax consequences—the investment gains would be tax free.

No Market Volatility: It is not just that they want this hypothetical investment to be dependable, ideally it would not be tied to the performance of the stock market. That way, if their other assets have a bad year, their "perfect investment" will still enjoy a predictable increase, which in this scenario would be all the more valuable.

Yields Income Besides Capital Gain: The perfect investment would provide cash flow over time, beyond its simple market appreciation in value.

Creditor Protection: It is one thing to focus on the safety and guarantees propping up the market value of the asset we own, but to make it even *more* desirable the owner would enjoy creditor protection. In other words, if the owner got into trouble elsewhere, and owed outsiders more than he could pay them, these creditors would *not* be able to seize his "perfect investment."

Inflation Protection: This is similar to "no market volatility." Just as investors would not want their hypothetical asset to drop when the market crashes, they also want their perfect investment to keep pace with price inflation.

Control: This is related to "liquidity." People are very familiar with investments they have no control over; their money is being held by others and is effectively in prison, perhaps for decades. The ideal investment would not be locked up behind onerous penalties for "early withdrawal."

Transferable: If desired, the owner would be able to easily transfer ownership of the perfect investment to someone else.

Easy to Manage: There should not be a big "learning curve" to figure out how to make decisions with the perfect investment. Not only does the owner want to be in control, but that control should not come with headaches.

No Hidden Fees or Penalties: Many people have been burned enough times by institutional money management firms that promote impressive rates of return in their brochures, without making it clear how much of those returns are absorbed by the management fees. The perfect investment would be very transparent, so the owner would never be surprised by money taken off the top.

Reputable: It goes without saying that in addition to all of the attributes we have described so far, it would also be ideal if the investment was reputable.

Private: The perfect investment would also be private. Investors would not receive a T5 tax slip itemizing the dividends, interest, or capital gains earned during the year, explaining the performance of their investment and otherwise telling nosey authorities about their business.

Tax-Free Wealth Transfer at Death: If the owner died before getting a chance to complete the investment, a death benefit, in the form of a cheque payable, *equalling the amount of the completed plan*, would bypass their estate, ie., it would speed things up tremendously, and be paid directly to their beneficiaries, *tax-free* within weeks. It, too, would be *protected from creditors* after death.

All the above attributes come pretty close to describing a dividend-paying whole-life policy. Does this all sound too good to be true? We have all been conditioned to accept bad news, while being skeptical of good news. But these are the attributes of an IBC plan, which anyone can check out and verify. And these attributes do not even touch on what you can do when you become your own banker. What I have just shown you is merely the *platform* on which an IBC policy is built. The real value comes with what you can do with it. That makes this perfect investment more than just a life insurance policy. We are talking about a concept—an idea conceived in the mind, using this platform. "Thinking like a banker" is the *process*, while life insurance is the *platform*.

UNDERSTANDING TWO MAIN TYPES OF LIFE INSURANCE

Life insurance is usually the last thing most people want to talk about—*unless* a loved one has recently died, and their family "thinks" they had life insurance. Admittedly, it is not sexy. But I would like to remind you that everyone of us dies.

Most life insurance is not *life* insurance. It is *death* insurance. Let me explain. Most of the life insurance in force in Canada is group term insurance, which is part of an employer's plan for their employees. This is a good thing because sadly, many people, even though they want it, would never have life insurance if it were not for group insurance. As an employee, a deduction is taken from your pay to cover your employee benefits, one of which is term life insurance. The amount of insurance coverage is limited and is only in force while you work there.

Surprisingly, many people do not know what coverages they have. If something happened to them and they had too little, they would be leaving their family in a financial mess. With group insurance, the employer is the policy owner and therefore has absolute control over it. Term life insurance is "death" insurance. There is *one* purpose to it—a payout on death. The employee does not own the policy on which the contract is written, and it is only in force if the employee is working for the employer. This usually means the employee is in good health and the risk of death is minimal. If the employee leaves the employer, the coverage normally ends. Alternatively, the insured can initiate a rewrite of the policy, at a much higher cost, based on the insured's older age and health status.

That is one type of term insurance. The other type of term insurance is what you buy on your own from an independent advisor, where you are the policy owner. Most people are familiar with this because it operates much like other types of insurance (car, fire, home, etc.). Term insurance covers you for a length of time. For example, if you take out a 10-year-term life insurance policy, the insurance company will quote you a level cost for the entire ten years. When the term period is up, the monthly costs increase because the insured is now ten years older. Term insurance premiums increase dramatically when the term is renewed, as I will demonstrate with Brad's story below, and lasts up to age 85, then it terminates. Hence, its name.

You most likely know much more about term insurance than the type of insurance that is used for IBC. Term insurance is "inexpensive" in the early years, and again, fills *one* purpose: a death benefit (i.e., death insurance).

THE STORY OF BRAD

The idea that term insurance is *"inexpensive"* can be deceiving since the older you get the costlier it becomes. Let's take an example of $250,000 of life insurance, which, by today's standard, is a small amount for a family, but for purposes of illustration it is all relative. The insured is a healthy 40-year old male, named Brad. He is a non-smoker. Why do I mention non-smoker? Because for people who smoke term insurance rates can more than double and triple!

Let's go for the cheapest form of term insurance for Brad. It is called, "Renewable and Convertible Term 10." This means the premiums will stay the same for 10 years, then increase to the next premium level. It also means it is convertible to permanent insurance (the cash value kind) at any age up to 85 without evidence of insurability. But Brad is not interested in any of that because he wants the *"cheapest"* life insurance.

In the chart below, you can see the insurance has an annual cost of $267. Very affordable! Brad feels his loved ones are protected if he dies. Ten years goes buy and Brad is still alive at age 50. So, now Brad gets a notice from the insurance company that his premiums have jumped to $1,396 per year! Brad is shocked but remembers his advisor told him the rates would increase to this cost. The costs are still affordable, so Brad takes the insurance for another 10 years.

Over the next 10 years Brad does not die. He reaches age 60 and gets a notice in the mail that the insurance company now wants him to cough up $3,363 per year! Humm.... Not good news. Brad sits down with his wife, who he has been married to for decades, and says to her, "If I died, you would be okay, right?" She says, "What are you talking about?" Brad explains that when he bought his life insurance the company charged him $267 per year, then it went up to $1,396 per year, and now they are charging him $3,362 per year!

Brad's dilemma is that if he takes the money and puts it toward his retirement he will have an extra $3,362 per year to invest, which would total $33,620 over 10 years. But if he dies, his wife is still not secure. Yes, their kids are now out on their own barely, but like most people in their 60s, Brad and his wife still carry debt and do not yet have their retirement ducks in a row. When Brad originally bought the life insurance, he was told by the advisor that he should not need the insurance at age 60, because he would have so much money in his mutual funds, he could self-insure. But Brad's retirement funds are not "in the bag" yet since the market has seen some vicious swings in the last 20 years.

Brad decides to keep the insurance and does not die. At age 70 the premium notice Brad receives indicates that Brad should keep his valuable life insurance coverage. When Brad looks at how much the premium has gone up he nearly has a heart attack! Now, the annual premiums are $10,342 per year! Brad does not even sit down to discuss it with his wife. They are both retired and there is no way they can afford to pay that much for the insurance. He promptly cancels it. Who would pay $10,342 per year and hope to die to collect on it?

Brad knows his wife will survive financially if he dies, but she would need to cut back on the lifestyle she has become accustomed to. She would receive a smaller income from Brad's pension, and his CPP and

OAS income would stop. Brad also wonders how either of them would pay for a funeral if the other died. Still worried, Brad decides to buy $25,000 of pre-arranged funeral insurance for $340/month ($4,080 per year). It is quite a step down from the $250,000 life insurance, but it is better than leaving his family stuck with the funeral costs.

Brad calls his advisor who sold him the term years before and asks: *"Since everyone dies sometime, wouldn't it make sense to have some permanent insurance so that it is paid up now that we are retired?"*

The advisor explains: *"My company's philosophy is 'buy term and invest the difference.' I'm sorry your mutual funds didn't perform like they were supposed to. If they had done better, you wouldn't need the insurance at this point in your life because you would have had more than enough money for your wife to maintain her lifestyle without needing your Canada Pension Plan (CPP) and Old-Age Security (OAS) to get by on like you do now. And she would also have had enough to pay for funeral costs if the market wasn't so volatile."*

1% VERSES 100%

This is typical of what happens with most term-insurance policy holders. Only 1% of term insurance ever results in a claim. Thus, the profit margins are significant for the insurer. The truth is, everyone will die. Because of this, having "a term insurance only" philosophy, such as was recommended by his advisor, doesn't make as much sense as having some permanent insurance along with it—since there is always a cost to dying. One of the benefits of an IBC policy is that it is permanent life insurance. Suppose that Brad had been diagnosed with Cancer at age 70, and was told he had less than 5 years to live. Now Brad and his wife are torn: Should he keep paying for the (death)income insurance that is now costing them $10,345 per year? If Brad's mutual funds had not performed well, as was the case, it may be very difficult for them to make the premium payment each year. In any case, if Brad decides to keep the insurance, most of the income, for example, that Brad is receiving from his CPP he won't see, since it is now redirected to pay for his more-valuable-than-ever life insurance. With this type of insurance, in spite of the cost, Brad will never be the benefactor of it.

The major difference between term insurance and dividend-paying permanent life insurance is this: term insurance can be used *once*, the day you die—and, historically, 99% of the time it is *never* paid out. Whole life insurance, on the other hand, is 100% guaranteed to pay out. It can be used everyday as we have discussed and will always be there until the day you die—if the minimum premiums are met—even if you stop paying for it years earlier.

Forever Insurance

A retired veteran of the life insurance industry recently gave a stirring talk focusing on the emotional connection he had with his clients and the advantage of owning whole life insurance over term life insurance. During his working years he personally handed out over $60 million of death benefits to beneficiaries of the policies he sold. These were tax free life insurance payouts from what he calls "forever insurance". And these were only to the clients who passed away while he was working, many of whom were in their retirement years. There are still many millions more in death benefits to come when his living clients eventually pass on. That's a lot of dough! How important is it that when an advisor retires, or dies, that he has helped to create lasting legacies for his clients? This could not have been done with term insurance.

Many people are concerned with getting the best price for their life insurance and are not aware how long or how much it will payout. But when it is your loved ones who will be the benefactors – or not – of your life insurance buying decisions do you really want to short change it? If this is the case, then any online life insurance transaction will do, and your family can hope for the best. Your life insurance should last as long as you do. Term insurance still plays a big role in protecting your family or business but, the transaction should be done in part with "forever insurance" and using a trusted advisor.

Your life should not be treated like your house. Thus, life insurance should not be treated like your house insurance. While your house may never catch fire and you may never need to make a claim, you cannot say the same thing about life insurance. Someday we all die. The question is, will the coverage be in force?

Table 5. Term insurance vs. "a plain vanilla" whole life insurance, using (-1%) current dividend scale

Age 40 - 85	Term			Whole Life (Illustrated in ages 50, 60, 70 and 85)		
Policy Year	Yearly Premium	Cash Value	Death Benefit	Yearly Premium	Cash Value	Death Benefit
40 - 50	$267.00	0	$250,000	$5,600	$54,222	$290,268
51 - 60	$1,396.00	0	$250,000	$5,600	$143,221	$354,589
61 - 70	$3,362.00	0	$250,000	$5,600	$264,215	$445,148
71 - 80	$10,342.00	0	$250,000	$5,600	$436,080	$580,928
81 - 85	$19,975.00	0	$250,000	$5,600	$544,091	$760,717
Total Premium	$254,235			$252,000		

To make a point, I am comparing Brad's term policy to a *plain vanilla* whole-life (WL) policy showing a **1% lower** dividend scale rate than the current rate (see table 5). To be clear, this policy is **not** designed the way an IBC policy would be designed. It is **not** designed to *maximize* cash value or death benefit growth and there are no extras on the policy to help accelerate these benefits. The policy was designed to highlight the death benefit, rather than the cash value, as are most WL policies that I come across that are designed by traditional advisors. Yet, as you can see, the plain vanilla WL policy, still looks pretty good with ample cash value. Any extra premium deposit contributed, up to the limits imposed by the tax act, would have been icing on the cake, and most of it would have gone directly into the cash value, providing more tax-exempt growth, while at the same time increasing the death benefit. This is where you would normally see exponential growth. Still, you must admit, that *plain vanilla whole-life policy looks enticing.* When you see later how we design it as an IBC policy, with its early accessible cash values, tax advantages, death benefit, and other guarantees, other investments have a hard time measuring up.

From table 5 you can also see:

1. If Brad had kept the term insurance until age 85, the costs would have *exceeded the cost of the whole-life insurance,* yet he would have no cash value to show for it.
2. The death benefit of the term insurance *stayed level at $250,000.* The whole-life death benefit grew to *three times more than the term insurance, totaling $760,717.*
3. If Brad had paid the term insurance until age 85 and lived, he would have paid *more premium* than the term insurance would have paid in *death benefit!* On the WL side, the cash value doubles per dollar of premium at 85—*and this projection is illustrated at **minus 1% lower** than the current dividend scale is at today for every one of those 45 years projected!*
4. The term insurance has no cash value. The WL policy would have accessible cash value. In this plain vanilla WL you have almost recovered your premium deposits in the tenth year of the policy, and the life insurance has increased by $40,268 from the original $250,000 of coverage it started out at. As you will see in the following pages, a properly structured IBC policy will perform considerably better.
5. Advocates of "buy term and invest the difference" (meaning you should buy the term insurance and invest the balance of what the WL premiums would be into an alternative account) all insist you can do better that way. As you can see in table 6, to do better than our plain vanilla WL, the alternative account would have to earn **8.44% compounded annual growth rate (not average return) with management fees of 2%, and tax at 25%, every single year for 45 years with no down years, just to *match* the life insurance cash values.** Remember, the WL has been projected at 1% below what its current dividend scale is today. Where are you *ever* going to find CAGR of 8.44% over the next 45 years with no down years?

Table 6. Comparison of $5,600 invested per year into WL insurance vs. "buy term and invest the difference" over 45 years

LIFE INSURANCE: RENT OR OWN

Owning term insurance is like renting a house; you pay rent every month to the landlord, who owns the property, for a month's worth of living space. You may do this for many years, but while you are never building up equity or ownership in the property for *yourself,* you *are* doing it for the *landlord* who is putting your payments towards the equity he or she has in it.

On the other hand, if you take out a mortgage to *buy* the house, then with each payment you are gaining equity in the property. Instead of getting one use out of every dollar and it's gone, you are now getting three *uses of every dollar:*

1. You have a living space,
2. You are building an asset, rather than paying an expense, which is what rent is, and
3. You can use the equity in the house for financing a second property if you so desire! Since you will need living space for the rest of your life, it makes sense to own.

Sound familiar? Let's draw the parallels. With a properly structured IBC policy you are also getting *three uses out of every dollar:*

1. You are getting a death benefit,
2. You are building an asset, rather than paying an expense, which is what term insurance is, and
3. You can use the equity in the policy for financing, to buy a property if you so desire! The difference here is now you are benefiting from your own system of financing instead of the bank's!

If your need for more life insurance coverage exceeds what the IBC policy offers, a "term insurance rider" can easily be added to your policy. If you have a growing family your need for life insurance will be high, as will your need for financing. When years have gone by and the "term insurance rider" renews at that much higher of a premium, you can drop the rider, and the whole life *will still be in force.* Usually by then, the WL death benefit coverage has grown significantly and exceeds the death benefit of the original term-insurance rider. Thus, you will still have insurance coverage later in life without paying the high renewal costs of the term insurance.

Most IBC policies are fully paid up in 7 to 9 years and do not require additional deposits to keep it in force. But you should keep making deposits. If every dollar you are depositing increases your cash value by more than a dollar, or doubles, or triples, or quadruples your dollars each year when doing so, then why would you want to stop?

ADDING A PUA RIDER

To increase your cash value growth so that it will *surpass* your deposits early in the life of the policy, we add a powerful growth-stimulating rider called *Paid Up Additions* (PUA). This makes all the difference. When you add this in combination with maximum additional premiums, the result is nothing short of amazing!

For those interested in the technical stuff, this is how it is defined: *Paid-up additional insurance is available as a rider on a whole-life policy. It lets the policyholder increase their living benefit (i.e., cash value) and death benefit with no evidence of insurability (i.e., no medical test or questions). In turn, PUA helps build your cash value very quickly, as the additional insurance earns the policy's guaranteed rate, plus dividends, and the value continues to compound indefinitely over time.*

So, while PUA increases your death benefit by definition and it is forever increasing, it simultaneously accelerates your cash values. How? By contractual agreement a whole-life policy's cash value *must* equal the death benefit by age 100. This amazes most people once they understand it.

Remember, the policy is a *contract*. For the cash values to close the gap between the ever-increasing death benefit (and the cash value amounts), the cash values *must increase more each year* to satisfy this requirement. When starting out, the death benefit is naturally much higher than the cash value. *At age 100 they must be equal.* So, the longer the contract is in force, the higher the cash values need to increase to close the gap.

WHAT DOES AN IBC POLICY LOOK LIKE?

Let's say we have a 35-year-old male whose goal is to *think like a banker* in order that he can be his own source of financing during his accumulation years, while stockpiling cash for income during his retirement years. He wants to build wealth of over $1 million by age 65 to supplement his retirement income, and of course, he wants life insurance protection. As shown on table 7 below, he deposits $20,000 per year for 20 years, then $15,982 for the following 10 years. No further deposits are made after that. The reason the deposits decrease between the twentieth and thirtieth years to $15,982 is because the 20-year term insurance rider needed to maximize his deposits in the beginning has been dropped, and thus the maximum deposit option reflects the limits set out by the exempt test policy (ETP) rules restricting how much can be put into the policy.

For starters, we are using a combination of whole life and term insurance making his premium deposits flexible enough, ranging from $5,000 to $20,000 per year. We are using the *current dividend scale* of a major insurance company *minus one per cent (-1%).* Flexibility is important because life happens, and some years are better than others. If our guy finds he cannot make the deposits he can lower them or put his policy on automatic premium loan where his insurance costs are drawn from the cash values (CV) to pay for the death benefit (DB). If necessary, he can cancel his policy and take the CV since there are no surrender charges like there are on universal life (UL) policies.

The values shown on table 7 show high CV growth. Observe that **at the end of year one** after depositing $20,000 his CV is $17,060, which is accessible, and his death benefit, which started out at $600,000, is $676,270 at the end of the first year. Thus, the PUA rider increased the insurance by $76,270 in the first year alone.

By year five, he has practically recovered all his premium deposits made over the previous five years, and his life insurance coverage has now grown to $979,985! His deposit was $20,000 that year, but his CV increased by $22,411 giving him a total of $99,700. Dollar for dollar of deposit that year, he got back 112%.

By year ten, his CV has grown leaps and bounds to $231,070, which is $31,070 more than all of his deposits totaled. His life insurance coverage has more than doubled and is now $1,351,267! He still made his deposit of $20,000 but his CV increased by $28,947 that year. In other words, for every dollar of his year ten deposit, his CV increased by 145%.

In year twenty, he has deposited a total of $400,000 and his CV is $593,667, and now his death benefit is $2,063,799. His CV increased that year by $43,565. That's 218% more than his deposit!

At age 65, he has put a total of $559,825 of his hard-earned money into the policy. He has $1,152,061 in CV, $2,268,498 in death benefit and his CV increased by $66,388 that year—more than four times his deposit.

And let's not forget that during the accumulation years he was surely using his CV for financing auto purchases and real estate deals so he could get multiple uses out of every dollar. He has more than likely recovered untold amounts of "lost-opportunity costs" (from either not paying interest to lenders for using their pool of money or losing interest by not having his money constantly working for him had he paid cash) over those thirty years.

Now he has reached his goal. How does he access the funds? In other words, he wants to (legally) avoid paying tax on the money he needs for his retirement. He also wants to keep his DB and leave a tax-free legacy for his family. And, he does not want to interrupt the "eighth wonder of the world" by stopping his CV from compounding. The laws in Canada state that any *withdrawal or policy loan* over the *adjusted cost base* (ACB) will result in tax payable to CRA. So, it makes sense to leave the CV intact *inside* the policy.

Although this is covered in Chapter 7, it bears restating. Rather than withdrawing the money or taking a policy loan, he can use his $1,152,061 CV as *collateral* for a line of credit for a bank loan from a major bank, where the borrowed funds are received *tax-free* and the outstanding loan is not repaid until the insured passes away. Caution should be exercised here and discussed with your advisor since these terms will differ with each collateral assignment.

Since this is a whole-life policy and the CV cannot go backwards, some banks today may lend up to 90% of the CV. Of course, when accessing funds this way for a tax-free loan, you will pay interest on the borrowed funds. Caution must be exercised here so that the interest charged by the bank does not exceed the cash-value growth of the policy. In other words, the borrowed amount should not trigger interest charges that exceed the expected cash-value growth of the policy.

If the insured passes away at age 85, his CV has grown to $2,588,523, and his DB is $3,257,184 to pay off the bank loan, and the remaining DB goes to his beneficiaries, tax-free. The government does not see one red cent of that money. I call that a win-win-win situation.

Notice at age 100, the CV and DB columns are equal (both are $4,240,660) to meet the policy's contractual obligation. Although you may not expect to live to 100, the CV growth during retirement years is at an all time high since it must meet this obligation.

Table 7. Premium deposits showing cash value and death benefit using (-1%) minus one percent current dividend scale as of 2018 from one of the major Canadian life insurance companies

Year | Age	Total Annual Premium	Total Cash Value -1% Current Dividend Scale	Total Death Benefit -1% Current Dividend Scale	Yearly Increase in Cash Value
1 | 36	20,000.00	17,060.97	676,270.20	17,060.97
5 | 40	20,000.00	99,700.18	979,984.46	22,411.87
10 | 45	20,000.00	231,070.29	1,351,267.40	28,947.27
15 | 50	20,000.00	395,034.08	1,711,667.76	34,445.42
20 | 55	20,000.00	593,667.42	2,063,799.95	43,565.55
25 | 60	15,982.52	843,933.03	1,914,133.09	54,565.39
30 | 65	15,982.52	1,152,061.51	2,268,498.90	66,388.85
35 | 70	0.00	1,435,783.74	2,485,640.76	60,233.47
40 | 75	0.00	1,763,739.28	2,721,901.47	69,285.47
45 | 80	0.00	2,143,942.87	2,978,545.16	81,075.58
50 | 85	0.00	2,588,523.14	3,257,184.80	92,314.21
55 | 90	0.00	3,058,105.62	3,560,163.23	93,796.18
60 | 95	0.00	3,526,169.61	3,888,050.45	97,341.63
65 | 100	0.00	4,240,666.29	4,240,666.29	212,685.39

These projections in table 7 are not overinflated. These are actual returns using today's current dividend scale from the participating account of the insurer used in this example *minus 1%!* For the small number of selected life insurance companies, we use for IBC, the standard deviation, or volatility, has been less than 3% over the last 25 years. When we compare this to the stock market, where the standard deviation can be as high as 16% over the same time period, life insurance dividend returns are very stable.

Besides stability, what about tax efficiency? The insured has not paid taxes on the growth of the CV and is able to access the money for retirement needs, tax-free! And again, the cash values cannot go backwards at any point in time, assuming he continues to pay his premiums deposits at least to when it *offsets* – which can be as early as 5 or 6 years depending on the dividends paid. This is an extremely solid asset to be in possession of. It is more secure than mutual funds, stock investments, and private equity where most RRSPs, TFSAs and non-registered funds are invested. On top of that, the money is accessible, and it has a death benefit.

Often, people criticize whole life insurance for not generating the returns that were promised. Unfortunately, this can be true if the policy is not structured for maximum results, and the advisor has not set it up correctly. Before reading Nelson Nash's book, and going through the process of certification, I was unaware, as are most advisors today, of the unique benefits a whole-life policy can offer when properly structured. There are a multitude of ways a whole-life policy can be structured to meet specific needs, and this is dependant on the needs of the client.

Most whole-life policies are structured for *insurance protection* instead of cash value. This can mean a significant difference in cash value. While insurance protection is important, "our need for financing exceeds our need for insurance protection" (Nash, 2000, 85).

PUTTING THE FOCUS ON CASH VALUE

When it comes to whole life, most financial advisors are trained to focus mainly on the death benefit and less on the cash value, except to say your cash value will pay your death benefit when you no longer need to pay premiums. Yes, the death benefit is *one* use. It will activated on the day you transcend this planet. But, it is in combination with the other uses that makes a properly structured whole-life policy so valuable as an asset and a living benefit. It is the other uses that make it the platform for the *Infinite Banking Concept. At its deepest level, IBC is about transforming the way you think about money, and how it flows into and out of your possession.*

Even though IBC is an abstract *process*, to practice it as Nash envisioned, it must be implemented on a tangible *platform*: specifically, a properly designed, dividend-paying whole-life policy. As Nash points out, there is nothing intrinsic to life insurance to connect it to IBC. It is simply the case that there is no better way of implementing IBC than using a life insurance policy of the structure I have been describing.

While participating dividend-paying whole life insurance is the platform, the policy's main uses, for the IBC concept, is to satisfy *financing* and *retirement* needs, as well as to provide a tax-free payout to your beneficiaries on *the day you die*! These are tangible values of owning permanent life insurance. Instead of buying term insurance—which is how most people have been taught to think about life insurance—it is far better to own whole life insurance for all the reasons I have mentioned.

CHAPTER

FOURTEEN

PARTICIPATING IN THE PROFITS: A WEALTH MINDSET

There are so many wonderful things that are readily available in this wonderful world, and financial prosperity opens the door to so many of those things. Most of us are spending our days exchanging our time for money, because money is essential to the freedom of life in this society. One of the principles we teach is to think from a *wealth mindset*, as taught by my friend Kim Butler, author of several books, one of which is *Living Your Life Insurance*. To do this, we must first examine our thoughts and beliefs about money. Are we living our lives with an abundance mentality or are our actions centred on scarcity?

For instance, if we believe there is more than enough, we will find ways to save, to give back, and invest in ourselves. However, if we believe we will "never have enough," we may paint a mental picture of ourselves with no money to spare, and literally bring it into reality by compulsively spending every penny we make.

What you practice mentally grows stronger.

As mentioned at the beginning of this book, you will be required to do your own thinking rather than letting everyone else do it for you. It is vitally important that you read and increase your financial literacy. This way you can achieve much more for much less time and effort. Every person faces financing issues, in some way, shape or form, at some point in their lives. Putting your financial future in the hands of the "experts" may leave you facing a headwind of debt where you are struggling in bondage decade after decade. Traditional financial advice fails to address these issues where continuous wealth transfers, in the form of interest payments, are being directed to banks and lending institutions when making life's purchases, such as for cars, homes, and business equipment. IBC is a process that when understood and acted upon rapidly eliminates these wealth transfers. The goal is to eliminate outside debt faster than any other method.

> *"You might be a redneck if you think life insurance is a Smith and Wesson."*
>
> — Comedian, Jeff Foxworthy

PARTICIPATING LIFE INSURANCE VS. BANKS

In our current economic climate, many are worried about the safety of their money. Dividend-paying whole life insurance is not tied to the market. In the 2008 market crises, all the companies we work with still went on to pay the same dividend as they did the year before and have seen only minor lower deviations in the years since. These were due largely to our low-interest-rate environment, rather than to a volatile stock market. Whether the market tanks or not, you cannot lose money in your whole-life policy.

As well, life insurance companies must have 100% or more reserves on hand at all times. The insurance companies we use have many times more reserves than required by Canadian regulations. When a person is issued a policy, the company already has the ability to pay the death claim. This speaks loudly to their ability to pay out dividends yearly, as well as their conservative choices for growing their capital over the past century. Canadian banks, on the other hand, have *less than* 10% reserves on hand, as required by the Bank of Canada.

POLICY LOANS VS. BANK LOANS

When you take out a policy loan, the insurance company charges interest that could be anywhere from 4.5% to 8%. The banks will also charge an interest rate which is usually much lower. The important viewpoint in this discussion is seeing yourself as the saver, the borrower, the banker, and the bank owner, versus seeing yourself as a consumer only.

Let's walk through the steps of taking out a loan, from the banks or other similar lending institutions, the traditional way and compare that with your own financing system, the IBC way. This excerpt is adapted from my friends Glen P. Zacher and Jayson C. Lowe, in their book *The Banker's Secret*, (2014, 85-87).

First, let's ask ourselves some questions about how we would get a loan in the traditional way using banks and other lenders, and who would profit by it.

THE TRADITIONAL WAY

1. *Do you have to fill out a credit application?* Yes. The credit application can be intrusive and annoying. You may or may not be approved depending on the bank's assessment of your financial state. Your credit score may also be affected every time you ask for a loan.
2. *Where are the funds borrowed from?* The funds come from the bank's pool of money.
3. *Where do the loan repayments of principal and interest get deposited?* To the bank.
4. *Does interest charged on loans positively impact the profits earned by banks?* Yes!
5. *Who participates in the earnings of the bank?* The shareholders.

Alternatively, let's look at what happens when the owner of a participating dividend-paying whole-life insurance policy, takes a loan against his or her own pool of wealth that has accumulated inside their policy.

THE IBC WAY

1. *Do you have to fill out a credit application?* No, it is your money. You fill out a "request for policy loan" and email it to your advisor, or to the insurance company, and your funds are directly deposited into your bank account.
2. *Where are the funds borrowed from?* From the participating account, which is totally separate from all other assets of the insurance company.
3. *Where do loan repayments of principal and interest get deposited?* To the participating account.
4. *Does interest charged on policy loans positively impact the profits earned by the participating account?* Yes!
5. *Who participates in the profits of the participating account?* Participating policy holders, and since YOU are a participating policy owner you get a portion of the profits.

The word "participating" in life insurance terminology implies accreditation and ownership. Once a dividend is declared it cannot be reversed. This is one of the guarantees of the life insurance contract.

CHAPTER
FIFTEEN

ARE YOU ON THE PATH TO FREEDOM?

To many people, achieving financial freedom is, or would be, the Holy Grail in life. We would all like to achieve financial freedom at some point in our lives and feel the rush of knowing that we own our future, by having enough money to live out the rest of our lives doing what we want, when we want, with who we want. Call it retirement, your golden years, but perhaps you want to simply call it financial freedom. You have finally bought your time back and every weekday is a "Saturday."

Unfortunately, very few people are on a path that will get them there. The vast majority are on a trajectory where they will instead reach old age living a seriously diminished lifestyle—or at best, having to continue working far longer than they would have anticipated because they have no choice. This concerns me! These people only "wake up" when it's too late!

If you are not getting ahead, where are you getting your financial advice from? What kinds of books are you reading? What are you doing to benefit your personal economy? Are you engaged enough in making this part of your life a priority? Are you planning to fail by failing to plan? Like a ship without a rudder, if you let the winds take you wherever they take you, you will end up… who knows where! It is true that most people have a *stunning disregard for planning*. Do not let this be YOU!

JOAN'S STORY

Perhaps a story will help. Joan (not her real name) is single, 74 years old and in good health. She may live well into her eighties or even nineties. She and her ex got divorced 20 years ago. In her settlement, she ended up with the house, worth about $345,000 today, which still had a significant mortgage remaining. Today she has about $93,000 remaining on the mortgage, approximately 10 years left, and is working in retail as a sales clerk. She is in fear of losing her retail sales job. She has had many jobs, from working in a farmer's market to various retail positions. She thinks, because of her age, she has been passed over for full-time work, seeing younger employees get the jobs instead.

Joan's income from both the Canada Pension Plan and Old Age Security totals $1,521.29 per month. Fortunately, this is indexed with inflation. Income from her retail job adds another $1,100 per month, giving her a total monthly income of $2,621.29. Her mortgage payment is $886.64 per month and property taxes are another $249 per month, totalling $1,135.64. You can see what she is facing every day with such a low income. Each month she has only $1,485.65 left to cover her heating, electricity, groceries, gasoline, car, house insurance, cell phone, internet, etc., not to mention gifts for grandchildren and savings for emergency in case the furnace or car quits. She also has two dogs and three cats that are costing her extra money to feed, but you will never convince her to give them up.

Soon, Joan will be forced into making decisions she would rather not make. She may have to sell her house, which needs repair, and buy a smaller house or condo. She could also start a reverse mortgage on her existing house which would give her extra income and take pressure off her needing to work.

No one wants to live out their retirement years with just enough to get by on. She would love to travel, since she is certainly healthy enough, and to have nice clothes and to not have to work, but these are not really options.

Joan is an advocate to her children and grandchildren these days, to plan early and to not make the same mistakes she made.

IT IS HARDER TO SAVE FOR RETIREMENT IF YOU ARE A WOMAN

During their working years, most women earn less income than men. Hopefully, that truth is changing for the better. Rob Carrick's article in the Globe and Mail in May 2018, showed that because women earn less than men on average, and more often take time out of the work force to raise children or look after elderly parents, they are not developing the same retirement income base. If you are not working, you are not paying into work pensions and not paying into CPP.

Women also have a longer life expectancy, which makes it even harder to save enough. Table 8, below, shows the average numbers of years of life expectancy at different ages for "healthy" males and females. The numbers of course will vary, with some living both longer and shorter.

The article estimates that women need total savings that are between 8.5% and 9.5% more than males, just to make up for their longer life expectancy. As well, a young woman who has recently graduated from a college or university would have to save 18% of her income to be as well off as a man in a similar position who saved 10%. That is due to women generally working fewer years and receiving fewer salary increases.

Married women have got to be sure they have enough to live on if their male spouse dies before them. It is rare to see male partners outliving their female spouses. A quick glance at my three widowed neighbours confirms this. In the last three years, three of my neighbors, who are all 70-plus, lost their husbands, all within a year and a half of each other. Surprising? Not really! Heartbreaking? Yes!

MY NEIGHBOUR LAYNE

I was relating this to my recently *retired* neighbour Layne. Layne is a great neighbor and his place is pristine! He is always working on his house or yard. But he found our conversation about all the neigbours we've lost recently rather disturbing. The first to go was Ross, who was my wife's and my next-door neighbour. After Ross' death, his widow Evelyn, found that she had more time on her hands, and became closer friends with Nel across the street. After a year or so, Nel's husband, Terry, died too. Then both Evelyn and Nel as widows, with more time on their hands, became close friends with Joanne, Nel's next door neighbour. After only several months Joanne's husband, Len, died also. Now Evelyn, Nel, and Joanne, with more time on their hands, have become closer friends with Debbie. Debbie is Layne's wife.

Thankfully, all these recent widows still had good retirement incomes. The worst possible outcome is for someone to outlive their money. The biggest fear in retirement is not being diagnosed with cancer or some other life-threatening disease, or even a terrorist attack. It is the possibility of outliving your money. I assured Layne that Debbie's income would continue if anything ever did happen to him since he still had life insurance along with a joint and survivor pension plan. This didn't seem to bring him the relief I thought it would. I could see a pattern was starting to formulate in Layne's head.

Table 8: Life expectancy differences between men and women

The difference in life expectancy between men and women

Women live longer than men on average, which is a big reason why they need to save more for retirement. Here's a look at life expectancy for women and men at various ages.

IF YOU'RE THIS OLD...		YOUR AVERAGE REMAINING LIFE EXPECTANCY WOULD BE THIS MANY YEARS*	TOTAL AGE
50 years	Males	32.0	82.0
50 years	Females	35.4	85.4
55 years	Males	27.6	82.6
55 years	Females	30.8	85.8
60 years	Males	23.3	83.3
60 years	Females	26.3	86.3
65 years	Males	19.2	84.2
65 years	Females	22.0	87.0
70 years	Males	15.4	85.4
70 years	Females	17.9	87.9
75 years	Males	12.0	87.0
75 years	Females	14.1	89.1
80 years	Males	8.9	88.9
80 years	Females	10.6	90.6
85 years	Males	6.4	91.4
85 years	Females	7.6	92.6
90 years	Males	4.4	94.4
90 years	Females	5.2	95.2
95 years	Males	3.0	98.0
95 years	Females	3.5	98.5
100 years	Males	2.1	102.1
100 years	Females	2.4	102.4

Source: Statistics Canada

*2013-2015 data.

IS LIFE INSURANCE A WOMAN'S ISSUE?

Since 70% of baby boomer women outlive their husbands, life insurance becomes more of a woman's issue. Not only do women have longer life expectancies than men, they tend to marry men older than themselves. Thus, many can expect to be a widow for 15, 20 or even 25 years. Having permanent life insurance during this phase in life is a vital piece of the puzzle and can make all the difference. With death a certainty, making the insurance company pay also becomes a certainty.

The facts are clear; 70% of the time women are going to be beneficiaries of a life insurance policy. Go find a widow who is living well and one that is not living well financially, and the biggest reason is life insurance.

Men do not always die first, I am not saying that. And, I am not saying that having life insurance is less important for women. Not at all. Women are making more money than ever, which means they need more life insurance than ever!

Having life insurance on both spouses or having a joint first-to-die (JFTD) life insurance policy, designed to payout a tax-free death benefit on either of their deaths, with the money usually being received within a few weeks of death, is key, and is an efficient way to cover off the worry of the "what if" scenarios. One thing you do not want to have to worry about when taking your last breath is leaving your spouse, who you have been living with for many decades, in a situation nobody would want to find themselves in.

WHAT WILL YOUR FINANCIAL FREEDOM LOOK LIKE?

Stop for a second and think about your definition of financial freedom. What will your post-employment decades be like? When will you begin them? What activities will you engage in? Where will you live? How much income will it take? These are the seeds that some people take the time to plant, and others blatantly disregard. Like the old saying goes: If you do not know where you are going, then any old road will do.

Whatever that destination turns out to be, you will likely live it for a long time: especially for women. Hopefully, these truly are your golden years and some of your most enjoyable. With your time no longer traded for money, and you should have the freedom you desire.

Okay. You are set to retire. You and your spouse have a good retirement income, no debts, you're in excellent health, the kids are gone, and dog has died. Perfect! What are you going to do with all your time? Is it filled with something meaningful that gives you purpose? Perhaps you have a deep passion for something you've been putting off. Maybe you like travelling and now you can always get the best destination deals. Perhaps your grandchildren are your priority. Or, you spend time improving your golf game with friends twice a week. You've got to find something productive to do. Us humans are all about improving something. Perhaps you and your partner have taken up cycling to get into better shape, and now you have the time to really enjoy it and love the feeling of being in top shape. And you are planning your next holiday. You are healthy, wealthy and wise! Wonderful!

The reality is, many people, like Joan mentioned earlier, will *not* see these years as their most enjoyable and least financially taxing years of their lives. For a large portion of Canadians these years will be their most stressful. While they had decades to prepare for these years, they let them slip by. With their heads buried in the sand, they took the ostrich approach to planning. Then, with limited or no financial knowledge, they attempt to survive in a world created for them by government programs. As a result, they end up looking for part-time jobs after retirement.

They had a good younger life. They had good jobs or ran profitable businesses and were physically and mentally at their best. They had good incomes. They had the toys and new vehicles in the driveway with all the latest options. They even had holiday trailers, took the kids on yearly summer campouts and winter holidays in the sun. And along the way, *they did not have a solid plan – or failed to plan at all.*

It seems reasonable to plan, yet most people do not give much more than a passing thought as to how much it will cost them to live comfortably when they retire, and how they are going to arrive there.

While advertisers succeed in getting us to buy now and delay our payments, we delay our own planning for a few more years, and again for a few more years, thinking it will get done. *It will not!* We need to be coached by someone. The great Ralph Waldo Emerson said, "People are eternally grateful to those who help them walk to a quicker, swifter beat." Who is helping you? Who will you be eternally grateful to?

Your financial health is just as important as your physical health or dental health! If you do not take proper care of your teeth, you may end up eating your suppers out of a straw one day. If you do not take care of your wealth you may end up eating your suppers where …?

I am reminded of the hordes of people who for years faithfully contributed to their RRSPs and non-registered retirement funds by investing in the stock market; then they lost nearly half of it in the financial crises of 2008. It took them 10 years to recover their losses. But even greater losses occurred in the Exempt Market where lifetimes of accumulated wealth were lost and will never be recovered. Be careful who has your money.

ARE YOU SAVING OR INVESTING?

People use the words "saving" and "investing" interchangeably when they are discussing financial products. To many people, these two words mean the same thing. But, there is a distinctive difference between saving and investing. Your *savings* is money you do not want to lose, whereas the money you *invest* is subject to the risk of loss.

Remember when you were growing up and you wanted to buy something really badly, but you did not have the money? It could have been a bicycle, a baseball glove, or a pricy pair of running shoes your mom would not buy you. So, you took matters into your own hands and you *saved* your money. You did not want to risk losing your money. You wanted it safe from loss, and liquid, so that when you needed it you could access it. You may have put it into an interest account at the bank or under your mattress. But you knew it was safe and accessible. That is *savings*.

Investing is different. When you put your money into any type of securities, no matter whether it is in the stock market, mortgages, bonds, land development, or anything where you could lose your money, it is an *investment*. There is an implied risk. Money in your mutual fund may grow and have some very good returns, but it is always at risk for loss.

CHAPTER
SIXTEEN

WHOLE LIFE PERSPECTIVE FROM A CANADIAN BILLIONAIRE

While the middle class is entrenched in the belief of bigger payoffs with bigger gambles, wealthy Canadians know better. They haven't fallen for the more-risk-equals-more-rewards mindset and are less likely to look at risk-based channels to keep all their money.

In a letter dated December 4, 2012, to a large Canadian life insurance company producer, Canadian business magnate and billionaire, Jim Pattison wrote:

> *Through personal experience I discovered that life insurance has other assets in addition to protection of one's present or future family.*
>
> *The business world, I discovered, has an interest in Life Insurance. Much of the world's business is carried on by credit, and bank applications for a line of credit are accom-*

panied by, as a rule, a statement of affairs which requests information as to the amount of life insurance carried.

When I decided to open my first business which was a General Motors automobile dealership franchise at the corner of 18th & Cambie, I discovered a "Living Benefit" of life insurance, that of borrowing collateral.

When I approached the Royal Bank of Canada, the cash values in my life insurance policies were a valuable asset that the Bank manager used in determining whether or not a loan would be granted.

If it wasn't for the cash values in my life insurance policies, the bank may have decided against granting me the necessary capital to begin my first business endeavor.

I am certainly an advocate of life insurance as a vehicle to help a young person take advantage of business opportunities that may present themselves in the future.

I am grateful for the living benefit of life insurance.

SAFE MONEY WITH GROWTH

As the story goes, younger people can afford to be more aggressive and have stocks as part of their portfolio when saving for their retirement. If the markets tank, which they always do because of their cyclical nature, you will have enough time to make up for the losses.

So the story goes. But it may take much longer than anticipated—even decades— to make up for the losses. This is why most people choose more conservative fixed income options as they age, thus reducing their exposure to the stock market. So, what is the problem here? The problem is by the time they reach a certain age and want minimal exposure to stocks, they are not well diversified. Most of their funds are in equities and there is no place to put their money for safe growth, which is their priority by then. They can move to money market funds, or GICs, but at 1% per year they are sacrificing growth.

Let's say they can find a GIC paying 2.5% or 3%. But even if you could find one, the interest growth is taxed at your highest marginal tax rate. This will reduce the growth to about 1.5% to 1.75%.

This is not where anyone wants to be in their later years in life. Your retirement years may require you needing income for 30 to 40 years.

A BETTER OPTION

If you are going to be holding your retirement portfolio in fixed income type vehicles, holding them in participating whole life insurance makes better sense, where the growth throughout all its years cannot be taxed.

Starting this at any age (whether using your life as the insured or not), and stuffing your policy with excess deposits, up to the exempt test limit, will earn dividend payouts from the dividend scale declared each year. Even with lower dividend scales, you will still have safety and growth!

If you could get a *non-taxed* annual growth rate of anywhere from 2% to 5% real return every year at retirement (*a reasonable long-term rate of return inside a properly structured whole-life insurance policy after the costs of insurance*), then you have beaten the odds. Why are you now winning? *Everything in the financial world is compared with what everyone else is doing!* But, 98% of Canadians in the retirement age bracket are doing the exact opposite and looking everywhere to find a savings vehicle that will pay them 2% to 5% every year—and that is *before taxes, not to mention having their funds in a vehicle that has a tax-free death benefit!* For most Canadians, the answer is hiding in plain sight. Life insurance is a sensible place to warehouse your wealth. But someone must inform you.

Many pre-retirees are exasperated. Where do they end up putting their funds? Some will invest in high-risk just to achieve a 1% or 2% higher return than what they are getting. How do they end up there? Pre-retirees are eager to attend anything dealing with their next phase in their life:

retirement. So, they attend a nice evening seminar with snacks and drinks at a leading hotel in the city. They listen to a polished speaker promising high returns in their private equity investment. They tell you how unhappy and dissatisfied people are with their current portfolio's performance and that theirs is better. They will say it is a new company that was formed because so many investors were unhappy with their current investments. You hear the presentation. The new company cannot offer *guarantees*, but they tell you the company is "solid" and has a good reputation. The brochures are nice and glossy, showing a consistent return of 5% to 10% (or higher) each year, blah, blah, blah. Wow! You start thinking of what those higher returns could do for you, especially if you put higher amounts of money into it. How much better would your retirement look then? So, you switch!

This is what happens to many people who have been saving for years. Because their retirement is right around the corner they get anxious. All they see is regular and consistent returns and what it will do for their portfolio. They think it is safe, even though they are told it is risky. And in all fairness, many of these exempt market, private equity firms do deliver. But, just as many do not. Where I live, in Alberta, investors have seen more than their fair share of failures. Because of this, regulations were tightened to strictly limit entry to this market to "eligible" or "accredited" investors who can "afford to lose the funds invested." Still, many people could not afford to lose and did. My advice is to stay clear of these types of investments or invest only what you can afford to *lose!*

Would you invest in a market where half of the deals go sour, just to get two to three percentage points higher for a short term, than what you can get in a safe investment for the long term? Many people do! It does not make sense! To lose at this stage is your worst nightmare—and it does not have to be this way.

SAFE AND RELIABLE RETURNS

> *Any financial plan based on a hoped-for return in the stock market (or any other market, for that matter) is not a plan, it's a wish.*
>
> — Dwayne Burnell, MBA

Canadian insurance companies have been paying dividends non-stop for over 150 years. Historically, participating whole-life policies have paid dividends since 1848, which was before automobiles, and before the Toronto Stock Exchange was formed. They have the longest track record of consistent performance, less volatility than GICs, and have been relatively stable compared with many financial instruments and indexes. Your cash value is guaranteed to increase contractually every year. Best of all, these increases are locked in. So, at the end of the year when your policy gets a dividend, there is no messing around about who gets paid. It is YOU!

I cannot tell you what the participating account dividend rate is for any of the insurers we work with because they change annually. But you would be impressed. Owners who have these types of policies have seen consistent and predictable cash on cash competitive compounding returns year after year.

There are many additional benefits, such as no management fees, no withdrawal fees, tax-exempt growth, tax-free estate values, protection from creditors in case of a civil suit or bankruptcy. Outside investments would have to realize far higher, more consistent returns, and better protection, than what you can find anywhere today. Dividend-paying whole life is its own separate asset class, just like any other asset class, and more people are discovering its unique benefits for themselves.

THE FINAL CHAPTER

'TIL DEATH DO US PART

Death is a topic we do not spend a lot of time taking about. Hopefully, it will be a long time off before most of you will be facing it. And I'm sure most of you don't spend much time worrying about it. Yet, at some point we will have to endure it. Will it be peaceful? Will it be painful? Who knows? Each of us have our own thoughts on this. We tend to think more worrisome thoughts about *our loved ones* having to experience death than ourselves.

If it is the death of a loved one, we will be at a loss. Those who love us will experience a loss at our death. Yes, the grieving process is real and necessary whichever way we look at it: whether it is us who dies or someone we dearly love and will miss. If the death is due to an accident or suffering of any kind, we dwell on the suffering and how it breaks our hearts that someone we loved so dearly had to suffer so excruciatingly. Our grieving is much worse.

I recently had a very moving, yet bizarre, conversation with a dear, long-standing friend of mine. As we were sitting around a campfire my usually upbeat and energetic friend was telling me how one week before he had been in the hospital. He had been through weeks of confusion and memory loss. He was in a state of depression and could barely function. As a contractor with a thriving business, he happened to be out of town staying at a roadside motel when this started. His depression increased, putting him in a fog, as he sat in his hotel room not knowing what was happening. He called his wife and they talked for hours throughout the night. He could not just get up and drive home. He had a contract to fulfill. He made it through the next day through sheer willpower, taking it one hour at a time. All he could think about were depressing thoughts and wanting to die. My dear friend no longer wanted to live!

A few days passed. Home again, and doing smaller contracting jobs, he still could not shake the fog he was in, though some days were better than others. Nearly two weeks passed, and he and his wife did not know what was going on. He had lost over 10 pounds and was not overweight to begin with.

He finally called a close mutual friend of ours who is an emergency room doctor. Our doctor friend was working that night and told him to come see him immediately. Our friend asked him if he was taking any medication that could have brought this on? Yes, he had recently been prescribed Crestor from his regular doctor to keep his cholesterol in check. Our doctor friend recommended he stop taking Crestor because of a known side effect that can cause exactly what he was going through. Amazingly, within days of stopping the medication our friend started to feel himself again.

As my friend was telling me this a week after his ordeal, he told me there were times that the depression he experienced became so intense, and so unbearable, and so excruciating, all he could think about was wanting to die.

"I thought about my life insurance. Would it pay out if I committed suicide? At least my wife would be able to survive without me," he said. WOW! Imagine that. Thankfully, there is a good ending to this story and my good friend has regained his normal robust self again and feels great.

While we know that depression is real, and people do commit suicide because of its unbearableness, for my friend it was not alleviated by taking a medication for it—of which there are good medications—but by getting off another unrelated med that was causing it. To answer his question, yes, the suicide clause in his life insurance policy states that *after the first two years* the policy is in force, the death benefit will payout if the insured commits suicide. There have been other stories I have heard from friends and clients of experiences they have had that brought them face to face with death, whether from a serious car crash or health scare. The most prevailing and comforting thought they all had was knowing they had life insurance. They did not have to worry if their spouse or family would be okay. *They were more worried about their loved ones than about themselves.* That is how we roll, us humans! In my friend's case, even though his kids are adults and no longer dependent, it was his *spouse* he cared about. Way to go buddy!

This story is real for all of us. At some point we will pass. Whether this is comforting or stressful, there is no escaping or running away from it. We cannot hide, it will hunt us down. Are you ready for it, whenever it may be?

YOUR FAMILY LEGACY

Leonard Renier is the founder of the Wealth and Wisdom Institute in California. While once visiting the San Diego Zoo, he noticed every animal display had something in common. Each one of them had a plaque that said it was sponsored by a family or family foundation, a.k.a. generational family wealth. What did these families do? The revelation hit him like a freight train! These families leverage the least amount of money to create the most amount of wealth, by investing in their families! He discovered the rich have three basic rules that are the centre point of their financial success.

> RULE NUMBER ONE: In your family, use the least amount of money to create the greatest amount of wealth.

> RULE NUMBER TWO: Guarantee the wealth will occur and the legacy will transfer, tax free.

> RULE NUMBER THREE: Create multiples of wealth immediately.

That was the answer and the rules became clear. On the way home from the zoo, one thought kept echoing through his head: rich people think like rich people; poor people think like poor people. He asked himself one question. *Would someone want to create wealth for their family if they knew they did not have to spend one more dime than they were spending now? If you could realign your assets to increase your wealth, and still retain control of the money, would you do it?* The key, he thought, to all of this is to consider the family, the whole family, as a financial tool.

Financial success is about having CONTROL of how you are using your money to create wealth. In the old days, the family had control of the family farm. The family could affect the growth and future production of the farm they owned and controlled. Investing in stocks and mutual funds do not provide the ownership and control needed to pass on wealth successfully. You are affected by too many elements out of your control, such as tax, investment risks, creditors, and luck. Yet, traditional advice has reinforced this as the only way to create wealth.

USE LEVERAGE

Unfortunately, following traditional investment advice does not create multiples of wealth immediately. But as Leonard Renier asks, "If you were able to invest in an older member of your family and he/she allowed you to do so to create the ultimate family legacy, what investment would be used?" Life insurance. It is the perfect solution for family wealth creation. It is a contract the family CONTROLS. The cash value and death benefit grow tax-deferred and tax-free. It is protected from creditors and passes outside of probate. Any number of family members, including the parents, can contribute to the premiums.

"This is the greatest family legacy you can ever pass on to the family, using the least amount of money, and all of it is centered on the legacy of love," says Renier, adding:

> It will be a very emotional decision and should be viewed with the proper perspective. Think of the old days, all of the members of the family would invest all their time

and money to increase the wealth of the farm, knowing they would someday own it. It would be theirs. They did not do this out of greed, but out of love for the family.

This was the generational solution back then.

TODAY'S GENERATIONAL SOLUTION

For the generational solution to work, your family must be aware that this opportunity exists. Renier, in his 60s, gathered his family together for a family dinner. After dinner he told them he wanted to seek out every opportunity they had as a family to create real wealth. The goal was to spend the least amount of money to create the most amount of tax-free wealth without any additional money being spent.

He paused a second and told them: "Rich people think like rich people; poor people think like poor people. The difference between the two is that rich people insure and guarantee that their wealth will be passed on to their families tax-free." Well, the truth, he told them, is "most us are not rich." He said, "I would like to pass on as much wealth to you as I possibly can offer you." It was quiet at the table, and he said, "The opportunity to accomplish this is sitting right in front of you. I want to offer you the opportunity to invest in me. I want to do this out of love, as a family legacy for you and my grandchildren. This is the last gift of love I can offer you."

He told them they could do this without spending any more money than they were already currently spending. This would be their investment in the family. A family needed a vehicle that would give them tremendous financial rewards, utilize the least amount of money, and would pass the money to the members of the family tax-free. So his children, who were in their 30s, purchased a life insurance contract on his life with the highest paying death benefit, using the least amount of premium to fund it. To pay for this they stopped over-funding their company pensions, and retirement plans. Between his kids, this came to a nice sum of money. If he lived another 10 years, and the death benefit was paid (i.e., he died), the annual rate of return on their investment would be 36%

tax-free. If he lived another 20 years, the annual rate of return would be 18% tax-free. Even at the age of 80, his family legacy would create about $1.7 million for them tax-free, upon his death. His children would own the policy and have access to the values in it even while he was alive.

The value of life insurance cannot be overstated. In Renier's situation, the generational solution was simple in nature, yet created dramatic results. There are many ways in a family setting to create and fund a family legacy, and at the same time reduce future taxation. As Renier says, it also addresses the issues of a financial future that is filled with the uncertainty that younger people are facing today. This is not a trendy solution that fades as markets change; rather, he says, it is a solid foundation for creating wealth in the future. It reduces the amount of risk and future taxation that you would typically be exposed to. It is also possible that all of this can be achieved without spending a nickel more than what you are spending now.

Understanding the current economic trends and shifts that will impact your future will be an advantage to anyone in preparing for the future. With so many changes simultaneously affecting the market today, along with higher taxes, it is not the same economy our parents relied upon for their future. These are major concerns for this generation. Now, imagine Renier's idea of creating future wealth in a family and having it pass tax-free. Imagine, Renier himself, taking his last breath knowing his family would know their future was financially secure.

How would it change your life? All of this can happen if you understand a few simple lessons:

1. **Permanent dividend-paying life insurance:** This asset is vastly underutilized in this country. It has been used in the same capacity as mentioned above for 200 years, but only in the last 50 years has the trend been toward term life insurance. All life insurance purchased at one time was permanent life insurance. That was the original purpose of life insurance. Since everyone died, it was guaranteed to pay out. It had huge and wide appeal! Dynasties were created because of it. Now that most life insurance sold is term insurance, and it is

designed to terminate before you do, it is far less appealing, and far less of a generational life-enhancing solution.

2. **Leverage:** Wealthy people understand how to use the least amount of money to create the most amount of wealth. The difference between the rich and the poor is the rich know how to control and secure their wealth now and for the next generation, and to do it tax-free.

3. **Accessible and Liquid Wealth:** When you have access to wealth, opportunities find you. When you have no access to wealth, debt finds you. Nash goes further, saying, "When you have access to wealth, opportunities will *hunt you down!*"

4. **Recapturing Lost-Opportunity Costs through Uninterrupted Growth:** Using your own pool of wealth, to finance the things you need in life, feeds your system instead of the lenders.

5. **Control:** Unlike many assets today, with permanent dividend-paying life insurance you always have control.

6. **Safe and Reliable Returns:** Life insurance companies are some of the oldest and safest institutions in Canada. Canadian insurance companies have been paying dividends non-stop for over 150 years.

7. **Tax-Exempt Growth:** Each year you will have a big smile on your face when you receive your anniversary statement showing all the growth in your funds as "exempt from taxes."

Tax-sheltered insurance accounts are an excellent way of building assets for retirement. At retirement, borrowing tax-free income is a strategy that will maximize spendable income while avoiding benefit clawbacks and reducing or eliminating tax payable.

— Terry Laughren, Chartered Accountant, Saskatoon

THINKING LIKE A BANKER

There is no "one right way" to implement IBC. As each person and case is unique, careful discussion is required in designing each policy. For some, plopping in large premium deposits is appropriate because they want to have large amounts available for policy loans sooner and they have the funds available for this purpose, usually from other "investments" that are not producing the results they intended. Others are more interested in allowing the policy build up over several years before taking a loan. The common denominator for both types of individuals, however, is the same: They want access to their cash value, they want predictable annual tax-exempt growth, without risk, where they cannot lose the funds that have already accumulated, they want protection from creditors, and they want the unique function of tax-free intergenerational wealth transfer.

> *You cannot bring about prosperity by discouraging thrift. You cannot strengthen the weak by weakening the strong. You cannot help the wage earner by pulling down the wage payer. You cannot further the brotherhood of man by encouraging class hatred. You cannot help the poor by destroying the rich. You cannot keep out of trouble by spending more than you earn. You cannot build character and courage by taking away man's initiative and independence. You cannot help men permanently by doing for them what they could and should do for themselves.*
>
> — Abraham Lincoln (1809-1865)

APPENDIX

REFERENCE LIST

Burnell, Dwayne, MBA. *Financial Peace of Mind*. Financial Ball Game Publishing, 2010.

Butler, Kim D. H. *Busting the Interest Rate Lies: Living with Passion, Purpose, and Abundance Throughout Our Lives*. 2015.

Butler, Kim D. H. *Financial Planning Has Failed: Reject Typical Financial Advice and Create Sustainable Wealth – Without Wall Street Risks!* 2015.

Butler, Kim D. H., Douglas Guest and Antoine Rempp. *Live Your Life Insurance*. Canadian Edition, 2015.

Chandler, B. Chase, Douglas Guest and Antoine Rempp. *The Wealthy Physician, Canadian Edition, Learn the Truth About How Medical Practitioners Should Protect & Grow Wealth*. 2014.

Irman, Mary Jo. *Farming Without the Bank, Your Solution to Farm Finance*. Fiscal Bridge Publishing, 2014-2015.

Irman, Mary Jo. *Wealth Without the Bank or Wall Street, Your Next Step to Guaranteed Liquid Wealth and Tax-Free Retirement*. Fiscal Bridge Publishing, 2016.

Kiyosaki, Robert. *The Cash Flow Quadrant, Rich Dad's Guide to Financial Freedom*. Google Books, 1998.

Lara, L. Carlos and Robert P. Murphy, PhD. *How Privatized Banking Really Works, Integrating Austrian Economics with the Infinite Banking Concept.* Sheridan Books, 2010.

Lara, L. Carlos, Robert P. Murphy, and R. Nelson Nash. *The Case for IBC: How to Secede from Our Current Monetary Regime One Household at a Time.* Ann Arbor, MI: Sheridan Books, 2018.

Moran, Will, MA, CLU. *Become Your Own Source of Financing.* 2015.

Moxley, Richard. *The Nine Rules of Credit (Canadian). How to Start, Rebuild, and Always Maintain Great Credit.* 2012.

Nash, R. Nelson. *Becoming Your Own Banker, Unlock the Infinite Banking Concept.* Infinite Banking Concept LLC, 2000.

Nash, R. Nelson. *Building Your Warehouse of Wealth, A Grassroots Method of Avoiding Fractional Reserve Banking – Think About it!* Infinite Banking Concept LLC, 2012.

Poteet, Raymond and Holly Reed. *The Tree of Wealth, How to Build a Legacy.* Amazon Digital Services LLC, 2017.

Renier, Leonard A. *The Family Legacy, The Generational Solution, Creating Generational Wealth, Revised Addition.* 2018.

Shiels, Robert (Bob). *You Don't Have to Die to Win (Canadian, How to Make Life Insurance Work for You.* Opus House Incorporated, 2009.

Stanley, Thomas and William Danko. *The Millionaire Next Door, The Surprising Secrets of America's Wealthy.* Pocket Books, 1996.

Storelli, Alberto. *Guaranteed Income, A Private Banking System for Canadians.* 2014.

Yellen, Pamela G. *Bank on Yourself: The Life-Changing Secret to Growing and Protecting Your Financial Future.* New York: Vanguard Press, 2010.

Zacher, Glen P., CLU and Jason Lowe. *The Banker's Secret, A Simple Guide to Creating Personal Wealth for Canadians.* 2014.

VIDEO CLIP RECOMMENDATIONS

http://moranfinancial.ca/infinite-banking-concept.html

https://www.youtube.com/watch?v=Vl_AIQqozaM

https://www.youtube.com/watch?v=jASi9y-BqSk

https://www.youtube.com/watch?v=R4MMeFOO5qY

* Uses of the word "bank", "banker", or "banking", that is found throughout the chapters in this book, is NOT used to confuse with, or indicate or describe any part of any regulated banking businesses or institutions (accept where it is obvious, such as when referring to banks, chartered banks, trust companies, or credit unions) that exist in Canada as defined in the Bank Act of Canada, including any of its products or services or the means by which any of these products or services may be obtained. The words used here refer to a strategy conceived in the mind of Mr. Nash. They do not indicate or describe a business.

A DESERVING TRIBUTE

Standing here with the one and only R. Nelson Nash, whom I have met numerous times, I realize how he has been an unknowing mentor, not only to me but, to thousands of financial professionals and clients throughout his 60-year long career. Having "retired" in November 2016 at the age of 86, Nelson continues to be one of the most sought-after speakers year after year. As keynote speaker at the annual three-day **Nelson Nash Institute Think Tank Conference** held in Birmingham, Alabama each February, his keen sense of humour and powerful speaking style never fails to amaze audiences wherever he takes the stage.

Nelson does not ascribe to the word "retirement" and instead prefers to call these past almost 30 years, his "passive-income years." Until October 2016 Nelson travelled extensively around the United States and Canada – over 50 weeks per year – usually with his wife, of over 60 years, Mary.

Though banking has been around since biblical times and life insurance has been around longer than automobiles, Nelson saw, before anyone else took notice, that life insurance could be used for the purpose of becoming your own source of financing. In his book *Becoming Your Own Banker, Unlocking the Infinite Banking Concept* (IBC), he demonstrated how you could significantly improve your financial situation by running your dollars through your own private and personal monetary system.

Becoming Your Own Banker, now in its fifth edition, continues to gain popularity and momentum, as do his three follow-up books expanding on this subject.

Much of traditional planning involves linear thinking and transaction-based approaches and Nelson continues to challenge the status quo, and the talking heads in the media, whose careers, books, and messages to the world, are routinely focused on accumulation and net worth, mainly because the industries that back these products want it that way. This is little comfort to the guy or gal who is more concerned about the dollars they are paying for interest out of their pockets to banks, and other lenders, for the major items they need in life such as homes, cars, and business purchases—dollars they will never see again, and dollars that will never earn interest for them either!

The major issues facing individuals and businesses today is not accumulation and net worth, as advertisers would have us think, but financing and recovering the lost-opportunity costs associated with that financing. Nelson has led the way, but it is up to us to decide which path we will follow.

ABOUT THE AUTHOR

Will Moran, MA, HBA, CLU

Most of us have been taught since we were kids growing up that we should avoid debt and pay cash as much as possible. But have you ever stopped to consider the financial impact of paying cash? When you pay cash, you lose the interest that money could have earned for you. You are giving up what Albert Einstein called, the "eighth wonder of the world," *compound interest.*

But what if you could somehow earn interest on all the money you use when paying cash? How would that improve your wealth generating potential? What if there was a way you could buy the things you want and still earn interest on the money you used?

Debt can be the biggest detriment to you becoming financially free. Every year we hear that debt, for the average Canadian, is piling up and increasing each year. The average Canadian is spending more on interest payments for their mortgages, car loans, credit-card debts, and student loans, than they are saving for themselves. What if there was a way you could build a system that recaptures this interest and would quickly put you on the road to financial success?

We know that banks and lending institutions are making huge profits from all the interest they are receiving from their borrowers. But that's only half the story. Have you ever thought of how much money they make on all our deposits? When we start building our own private "banking" system, not only can we recapture the interest we would be paying to banks, but also the profits that they make on all of our deposits.

For most people, after having exchanged a dollar for a good or service, it means that dollar is spent, and it is gone. Like a 1980s cell phone, that can make a call, and nothing more, your dollar serves one purpose for you, and nothing more. The "Infinite Banking Concept" shows us how one dollar can do much more than one job. Just like today's smart phone does more than one job, replacing your GPS, iPod, pocket camera, calculator, newspaper, not to mention all the other functions it serves, so your dollars can do multiple jobs and serve many more functions, too.

Instead of doing one job and exhausting the use of that dollar, you can multiply its use by running your dollars through an asset that you own and control, thus getting an "infinite" number of uses from the same dollar over and over, while not losing its earning power, and all in a tax-free-growth environment!

We are not living in our parents' economy. What, if anything, has the financial services industry done in the past 30 years to improve the threatening debt ratio of the average Canadian? The Nelson Nash Institute is answering the call. The "Infinite Banking Concept," created by Nelson Nash, gives us the tools to take control over the financing and banking functions in our everyday lives. It allows us to change the direction our money is flowing. How much faster would your wealth grow if all of the payments you are currently paying to banks were now going in your direction?

Will is the founder and president of Moran Financial Inc. and Wealth Economics. For the past 25 years, he has focused on the personal finances of individuals and business owners. As a financial educator, he challenges the status quo, helping to cultivate a mindset where one dollar can do many jobs, where there is abundance as opposed to scarcity, and where, in the end, his clients discover a whole new financial world that works for them rather than against them.

Will was born and raised on his family's farm outside of Petrolia Ontario and was a police officer before attending the University of Western Ontario, and later the University of Alberta to receive a Master of Arts degree in socio-economics. Over the past 20 years, Will has been a speaker and business builder in both Canada and the US.

Will resides in Edmonton, Alberta with his wife, Sue, who works in the medical field as a sonographer. Together they have raised three children, now all adults, who they love spending time with. In his free time, if not reading, cycling, golfing, hiking, or skiing in the mountains with his family, Will enjoys vacationing with Sue and spending time doing the things they both love—exploring this wonderful world.

Moran Financial Inc.
10250A 176 St. NW
Edmonton, AB T5S 1L2
Phone: (780) 438-0763
Email: Will@MoranFinancial.ca
Web Site: www.MoranFinancial.ca
Web Site: www.WealthEconomics.ca

Made in the USA
Middletown, DE
09 July 2019